T0088682

THE DIAMOND SUTRA

TRANSFORMING THE WAY
WE PERCEIVE THE WORLD

THE DIAMOND SUTRA

TRANSFORMING THE WAY
WE PERCEIVE THE WORLD

Mu Soeng

WISDOM PUBLICATIONS • BOSTON

Wisdom Publications
199 Elm Street
Somerville, MA 02144

© 2000 Mu Soeng

Library of Congress Cataloging-in-Publication Data
Mu Soeng.
        Diamond Sutra : transforming the way
we perceive the world / Mu Soeng.
            p.   cm.
        Includes bibliographical references and index.
        ISBN 0-86171-160-2 (alk. paper)
        1. Tripiṭaka. Sūtrapiṭaka. Prajñāpāramitā.
        Vajracchedikā—Criticism, interpretation, etc.
        I. Tripiṭaka. Sūtrapiṭaka. Prajñāpāramitā.
        Vajracchedikā.
        English. II. Title.
        BQ1997.M8 2000
        294.3'85—dc21   99-36871

ISBN 978-0-86171-160-4
eBook ISBN 978-0-86171-829-0
15 14 13 12 11
7 6 5 4 3

Cover Design by Tony Lulek. Interior by Gopa&Ted2, Inc. Set in AGaramond 11/13.25.

Table of Contents

Publisher's Acknowledgment

THE PUBLISHER gratefully acknowledges the generous help of the Hershey Family Foundation in sponsoring the publication of this book.

Preface

A CAUSAL NEXUS of infinite complexity connects a barefoot monk dressed in rags in ancient India of sixth century B.C.E. to the great medieval monastic complexes of Todaiji in Japan, Songgwang-sa in Korea, and to the staggering variety of Buddhist-inspired consumer products and services at the beginning of twenty-first-century America.

The journey of what we call "Buddhism" has been quite unlike that of other religions. After dying out in its original homeland of India, it became the dominant religion of the rest of Asia. Buddhism has had no khalif or pope to enforce its edicts, nor was there a book of incontrovertible revelations. But it does have a series of texts or sutras that have inspired the devotion and allegiance of its many subtraditions. These texts purport to contain the teachings of the sixth-century B.C.E. Indian monk Siddhartha Gautama, known to history simply as the Buddha, the Awakened One. The *Diamond Sutra* is one of these texts that has been pivotal in shaping the transformation of Buddha's teachings in east and north Asia.

Different subtraditions of Buddhism have at times espoused conflicting visions of human beings and their relationship to the phenomenal world. Theravada, the sole remnant of the earliest historical layer of Buddhism, concerns itself primarily with the functioning of the individual mind and how to find liberation within the mind. The later Mahayana tradition, with a more complex inner architecture, has several graduated layers. The focus of the earliest developments in Mahayana, exemplified by the Prajna-paramita texts of which the *Diamond Sutra* is one, is on emptiness *(shunyata)* and compassion *(karuna)* integrated in the overarching concept of its teachings as skillful means *(upaya)*. Here the search for salvation is framed not in terms of individual consciousness, but in terms of a visionary cosmos and the place of individual consciousness in it. Whereas the emphasis in early Buddhism was on the individual consciousness knowing itself, in Mahayana the question is how the limited individual consciousness may be opened up to the potentially unlimited universal or cosmic consciousness.

The Mahayana modality of giving meaning to the part by opening it up to the whole has many parallels with postmodern modes of inquiry. Quantum physics and deconstructionist theory in art and literature, for example, share a strong sense that there are no parts separate from the whole. Each part contains the totality of its environment, and divorced from the totality it is nothing. Modern holographic quantum theory posits relationships not between specific electrons, but between each electron and the entire implicit order of which it is a full-bodied manifestation. Deconstructionist theory views written words, texts, and works of art as ciphers whose meaning depends on the context into which the reader or viewer chooses to place them. This commentary on the *Diamond Sutra* attempts to see parallels in contemporary modes of inquiry.

The *Diamond Sutra* and other Mahayana sutras are the artifacts of a sumptuous religious imagination that once had tremendous impact on the civilizations of China, Korea, and Japan, but which may now seem irrelevant to the postmodern reader. In highlighting certain parallels between the sutra and postmodernism, my aim has been to present the ancient Mahayana wisdom tradition not only as relevant to our own time and place, but also as a tool of inquiry that can enrich our lives.

The main inspiration behind this commentary on the sutra is my own training in the Zen (Ch'an) tradition. For me, Zen continues, through its creative use of *koan* methodology, to be the approach where linguistic deconstruction at its best works without any attempt at reconstruction. From a historical standpoint, the Mahayana wisdom tradition seems to anticipate the koan system's paradoxical use of language.

This commentary treats the *Diamond Sutra* as a progenitor of the Zen tradition. For me, as for most students of Zen, the *Diamond Sutra* and the *Heart Sutra* are inseparable. My need to understand the historical background of these seminal texts was the incentive to produce this sequel to my commentary on the *Heart Sutra*.[1] My attempt in both cases has been to avoid getting stuck in academic minutiae—I have no wish to turn this commentary into yet another doctrinal point of view. At the same time I have included a historical survey of the Mahayana to give the reader an overview. My hope is that serious practitioners of Zen and Mahayana find the background material useful and the insights into the sutra inspiring.

Different generations have discovered these ancient texts and reflected on them in new ways. We are beneficiaries of commentaries on the *Diamond Sutra* by some of the greatest scholar-monks in Mahayana Buddhism—Asanga, Vasubandhu, and Kamalashila—as well as commentaries on other

Prajnaparamita texts by great thinkers such as Nagarjuna and Haribhadra. In order to remain viable, the teachings are often re-expressed in the idiom of the times. Each new commentary, in the best of intentions, expresses a point of view and is in the service of the continuity and development of the tradition.

In our time there is a sense of urgency to understand the ancient wisdom traditions in the face of the explosion of information from many diverse sources. In earlier generations the opportunity to read and understand religious texts was the province of a select few. Today we travel in cyberspace on the information superhighway. Practically anyone can access the totality of information (and misinformation) gathered in the last five thousand years of human history with the click of a few keys on the computer. But perhaps today's deluge of information has produced its own crisis of identity. The challenge to understand who and what we are may be greater than ever before. Another challenge may be to inspire people to move from a totally information-based orientation toward the transformative integration of insights from the wisdom traditions with their own experience.

This translation of the *Diamond Sutra* is based on the original Sanskrit text as edited by Max Müller. I have also consulted translations from Chinese sources, notably the Kumarajiva translation from the Chinese, which is found in works by D. T. Suzuki and others. This text was also used in a commentary by Thich Nhat Hanh. I have relied on the translation from the Sanskrit original by Edward Conze, arguably the greatest Western scholar on the Prajnaparamita literature. I have borrowed freely from these translations in order to produce an easily accessible rendering for the modern reader. In doing so, I have tried to soften the impact of archaic presentation as much as possible, while retaining the essence of the Sanskrit original.

I am grateful to Venerable Thanissaro Bhikkhu for his continual support and invaluable advice as the book was being written. All errors of factual presentation and interpretation are, however, entirely my own. I am thankful to friends and colleagues at the Barre Center for Buddhist Studies for creating a supportive environment, where I wrote major portions of this book. My thanks go out also to David Kittelstrom and Samantha Kent, my editors at Wisdom Publications, for all their painstaking work in turning the raw manuscript into a publishable format.

A Note on Terminology

SINCE THIS BOOK is addressed to serious readers of Buddhist teachings rather than scholars of Sanskrit language, I have opted for phonetic renderings for all Sanskrit words. The diacritical marks, so central to a scholarly approach, have been omitted in favor of a more user-friendly approach. Sanskrit words such as *anitya* and *anatman* have been used even in places where Pali words such as *anicca* and *anatta* are more familiar in popular usage.

PART I

Early Buddhism and Mahayana

Although the origins of what we today call "Mahayana" may never be accurately traced, there seems to be a consensus that during the two centuries from 100 B.C.E. to 100 C.E. there arose within Buddhism a movement that eventually called itself Mahayana, the "Great Vehicle" or "Great Course." This new movement dubbed earlier Buddhist movements "Hinayana"—the "Inferior Vehicle" or "Limited Vehicle"—in order to distinguish itself from them. The adherents of the Great Vehicle claimed that the path of the bodhisattva, which it advocated, leads to supreme, perfect awakening or buddhahood, while the Inferior Vehicle leads only to sainthood or arhatship.

The European orientalists of the nineteenth and early twentieth centuries tended to see the appearance of Mahayana as a dramatic and cataclysmic rupture within the Buddhist church, along the lines of Martin Luther nailing his theses on the doors of the church at Wittenberg. Modern Buddhist scholarship, however, generally agrees that the Mahayana was a gradual, mitigatory, reformist impulse almost from the beginning of the formation of the *sangha*—the community centered around the teaching and personality of the Buddha. It may also be added that in reading the day-to-day experiences of Buddhists in medieval India in their heyday, this controversy does not appear as sharply cleaved as it has been made out to be in our own century. On the contrary, it appears that certain doctrinal positions crossed the Mahayana-Hinayana divide, showing perhaps that the inner lives of the early Buddhists were governed not by labels, but rather by religious experimentation.

Buddhists view the Buddha as a *mahasiddha*,[2] a person of great shamanic powers who forged a new direction in the history of shamanism by laying emphasis on the primacy of intention, on personal and social ethics, and on the phenomenology of mental processes. While attainment of shamanic powers was a continuation of the Buddha's yogic training, his insistence

3

on ethics and intention was a departure from the larger religious climate of the subcontinent. This view challenges the image created by nineteenth-century orientialists of the Buddha as a grim, puritanical, Calvin-like figure. Conze was the first European scholar of note, in the middle part of this century, to break the spell of "Buddhist rationalism" and argue that there was compatibility and coexistence of magic belief and Buddhist philosophy.[3] The reality of Buddhism at the folk level in all Asian societies has remained closely wedded to the shamanic/ethical paradox, where the traditional emphasis on personal and societal ethics has at times been marginalized by practices of mystery and magic.

Buddhism is not a monolithic entity. It is rather a tradition from which people who consider themselves Buddhists draw inspiration and to which they add as they respond to the problems of their lives, sometimes reformulating the doctrine in new ways to make it more relevant, sometimes returning to earlier principles when they seem to be timely or in danger of becoming lost. The tradition is thus a history of what Buddhists think and do.

Siddhartha Gautama, the prince of the Shakya clan who became the Buddha, was a product of his time and place. His was a time of extraordinary change in all fields of endeavor. Most of all, it was a time of fervent religious and spiritual exploration. The quest for mystery and magic was a prominent, even dominant, feature of this exploration.

In the centuries before the time of the Buddha, the Vedic civilization flourished through the leadership of the traditional aristocratic and religious elite in a clan- and caste-based agrarian society. As the eastward exploration of the subcontinent opened up new frontiers for Vedic society, it brought new challenges to the entrenched religious elite. The most potent of these challenges—intellectually and religiously—came from the rise of asceticism.

By the time of the Upanishads (circa 800–600 B.C.E.) asceticism had become widespread. It was through the ascetics, rather than the orthodox Brahmin priests, that the new teachings developed and spread. In those early centuries asceticism gave rise to an astounding range of experimentation, which continues to be a feature of Indian religious life today.

Some ascetics were solitary radicals or recluses who lived deep in the forest and inflicted austerities on themselves in order to become inured to hunger, thirst, heat, cold, and rain. There were also ascetics who embraced a less rigorous regimen and whose chief practices were the mental and spiritual disciplines of meditation. Some ascetics dwelt alone in the forested areas on the outskirts of towns and villages, while others lived in the forest in groups of huts under the leadership of an elder. A common activity of the life of the ascetics of the less rigorous regimen was to wander from village to village, either alone or in large groups, begging for food and clothing. The elder of the group typically had developed a religious doctrine of his own, which was proclaimed by the wandering group to all who wished to listen. Sometimes these mendicants entered into religious debate with other wandering ascetics. Some took advantage of the temperate climate to go naked, while others favored modesty and simple garments.

The rise of asceticism in India in the centuries immediately before the birth of the Buddha, spurred by the quest for magical power, was contextualized, perhaps even institutionalized, by the wandering ascetic *(shramana)* movement, whose members were a motley collection of primarily non-Brahminical spiritual seekers. These rebel ascetics sought magical power in order to compete with the Brahmin priests and scholars who already laid claim to social and political power by virtue of their caste and training. The Brahmins held power traditionally as the keepers of the cosmic mystery of fire sacrifices. It seems probable that, in the centuries preceding the Buddha, sacrificial mysticism had run its course and had come to be seen increasingly as a means of obtaining prosperity and long life. The Aryan civilization gradually moved eastward where Brahminism was less entrenched than in the west. And there, in the central and eastern part of the Gangetic plain, is where India's long adventure with asceticism began.

Asceticism, with its challenge to entrenched Brahmin priesthood as the keepers of spirituality and esoteric knowledge, allowed many from the underprivileged castes to enjoy success, rewards, and prestige that might not have been otherwise available to them. This challenge was much more viable in an expanding frontier society where the alienated and those seeking to escape the constraints of a highly stratified and ritualized Vedic society could hope to compete with the Brahmin priests on a more or less equal footing. The challenge was rooted as much in questioning the authority of Brahmin orthodoxy as it was in the search for mysterious magical powers. Throughout its long history, the religious culture of India, spurred by these twin desires, has produced its share of charlatans as well as authentic saints.

The greatest veneration in the emerging civilization of the mid-Gangetic valley was reserved, however, for those ascetics who had developed psychic faculties and gained insights that words could not express. These adepts were perceived as having plumbed the cosmic mystery, having understood the nature of the universe and of themselves, thereby reaching a realm of bliss unaffected by birth and death, joy and sorrow, good and evil. They were seen by their followers as having the magical power to crumble mountains into the sea, protect a great city, increase wealth, or wreak devastation if offended. In short, the magical powers formerly ascribed to ritual sacrificers were now transferred to individual ascetics. Their model was the great god Shiva, on whose appeasement depended the well-being of the universe. Like Shiva himself, an ascetic was considered a conqueror above all conquerors; there was none greater than him in the universe.[4]

At the time of the Buddha's youth, the definitions and goals of asceticism were firmly in place. The ascetic was searching for the six *siddhis* or "super-knowledges," such as the six found in this Buddhist enumeration: (1) magic powers (such as walking on water or flying); (2) the divine ear (being able to hear sounds from far away); (3) divine eye (being able to see things from far away); (4) memory of one's former lives; (5) knowledge of others' minds and thoughts; and (6) the extinction of the outflows, namely, sensuality, becoming, and ignorance. The first five superknowledges are shamanic powers, aspired to by shamans in every traditional culture, yet considered mundane by Buddhists who seek primarily the sixth super-knowledge. Only *arhats* realize the sixth superknowledge. For them, the first five powers are simply by-products, and all are ascribed to the Buddha as well as further results of his awakening. Interestingly, the divine eye and the recollection of former lives figured prominently in events leading up to the Buddha's final awakening, and in recapitulated accounts of his forty-five-year teaching career.

The Buddha's lifetime coincided with the development of new and enduring patterns of thought in Indian society. Michael Carrithers, a historian of Buddhism, summarizes these patterns thus:

> Their thought was symbolic, in the specific sense that it evoked or expressed—rather than questioned or explained—the shared experience and values of a relatively small-scale community. So long as that experience was shared, and so long as that community did not embrace too many disparate elements, there was no reason, indeed no occasion, for questioning the values.
>
> But with the rise of the cities and the growth of a complex cosmopolitan community, experience was no longer shared nor values unquestioned. The easy correspondence between traditional

thought and life no longer held. There were substantial changes in the forms of common life, and with those changes arose the possibility that those forms could be reconsidered, discussed and reasoned over; people could now philosophize over them.[5]

At the time of the Buddha, the agrarian society of the Aryans had given way to a new kind of urban/mercantile culture. City-states arose in the central Gangetic basin clustered around urban centers where there had been none before. Some of these were tribal oligarchies, some republics, and still others warrior states intent on conquest and expansion. These new centers of power became showcases for royal courts, for merchants and craftsmen with new skills, and a magnet for soldiers and laborers. Migrating populations, including foreigners, opportunists, and the displaced, flocked to these urban centers, while conquered chieftains came to the royal courts to pay tribute.

This newly emerging urban culture gave rise to novel financial arrangements, such as credit and debt, real estate speculation, and interest-bearing loans. These innovations challenged the entrenched caste system of the Aryan civilization since an entrepreneur of any caste could now accumulate wealth and power. Thus arose a new merchant-trader class with increased social and financial power. As pivotal members of the complex urban society, the newly prosperous city merchants found an affinity with Buddhism. It was this class that assured the spread of the Buddha's teaching and alms food for his monk-followers. (As a parallel note, it is worth noting the contribution of the Medicis and other merchants to the ushering in of the Florentine Renaissance.)

While Buddha's teaching found a strong resonance among merchants, especially those who traveled far and wide with their caravans of goods, it would be misleading to suggest that Buddhism had a monopolistic hold on the minds and wallets of the merchant class. Quite the contrary. The Jain order of monks, a tradition that often paralleled Buddhism throughout Indian history, also benefited enormously from the patronage of merchants. The merchant class, more than other sectors of the society, was exposed to a wide range of human growth and change, both physical and psychological.

The newly emerging urban/mercantile culture firmly subscribed to the idea of earning merit (or protection) through supporting monks, whether Buddhist, Jain, or Ajivika. The idea of "merit making" continues to exert a powerful hold on the imagination of Buddhists in Asia to this day. The symbiotic relationship between monks and laity through the exchange of material support and spiritual teachings continues to be a cornerstone of Buddhist continuity in Asia.

The monastic communities of the Buddhists, Jains, and Ajivikas were part of the larger *shramana* movement. The flavor of the shramana movement is best captured by the term *parivrajaka,* or homeless wanderer. The six-year ascetic apprenticeship of Siddhartha Gautama after leaving home at the age of twenty-nine took place within the culture of the shramanas, the renouncers of the world and all worldly entanglements. In a certain sense, the challenge posed by the shramana philosophers to Brahmin orthodoxy in ancient India has a parallel in the challenge by the philosophers of European "Enlightenment" in the seventeenth and eighteenth centuries to the orthodoxy of the Catholic Church. The shramanas rightfully have been called the first true cosmopolitans of ancient India. It is tempting to speculate on a possible connection between the words *shramana* and *shaman* although no etymological correspondence is to be found —the term *shaman* belongs to the Siberian group of languages, while *shramana* belongs to the Pali-Sanskrit group of Indo-European languages. However, the Chinese transliteration of *shramana* as *sha-men* puts it intriguingly close to the Siberian usage.

Historically and anthropologically, the terms shramana and shaman— while not linguistically related—have played an almost identical function in India and elsewhere. Contemporary anthropological research on neo-shamanism offers an intriguing parallel to Mahayana cosmological perspectives, as well as to contemporary thinking in quantum physics. According to a contemporary scholar of neo-shamanism,

> The "perverse" upside-down physics of the shamanic universe —in which time is stretchable, space is solid, matter is transparent, and conventional manifestations of energy are replaced by invisible subtle forces—cannot be grasped by our customary mode of perception. Nevertheless, all tribal societies as well as our ancestors—and cultures of both the Old World and our present world—did at one time subscribe to the idea of such a universe…[The shaman] speaks of the vitality of all that exists and of a global relatedness to all beings and phenomena at every level. To him the universe is pervaded by a creative essence which not only transcends normal existence but lends to it an inner cohesion. The shaman is part of the age-old tradition of the

Perennial Philosophy—the mystical teaching of the unity of all things and all beings. In the realm of magic everything is inter-related; nothing exists in isolation. Here rules the principle of *pars pro toto*. This level of consciousness, like a gigantic telephone exchange, affords access to all other levels of awareness. All mystical paths are agreed that such a way of experiencing requires a suspension of normal awareness and of rational thought by means of special techniques of mind training. An empty mind allows an alternative way of being and affords access to the existential level of transpersonal experience.[6]

We may find some support here for the thesis that aspects of Mahayana Buddhism are more deeply rooted in a pre-Buddhist, yogic civilization than previously thought. Asceticism, it would seem, was a driving force behind this yogic civilization.

The spiritual culture of the Buddha's time honored asceticism and renunciation:

> To be a renouncer was a young man's, indeed a romantic's aspiration, and from this point of view the Buddha was one of many youths who left home, attracted by the challenge of the wandering life. But the counterpart to this enthusiasm was a somber and deeply serious view of such a life's task. First, the refined ideals of virtue and wisdom laid upon these wanderers a burden of perfection which perhaps few could achieve in detail. And second, they left ordinary life not just because of its irritations, but also because of its dangers.
>
> The unexamined and uncontrolled life of the home leads only to sorrow and despair, endlessly repeated. Only the renouncer's life offers hope, the hope of looking down upon a morass of desire and suffering from an eminence of knowledge and dispassion. Western writers have often counted this view as unrelieved pessimism, but they have missed the optimism, the prospect of attaining "the deathless." The renouncers' attitude was compounded of dark bitterness and bright hope.[7]

As the first cosmopolitan citizens of the emerging urban civilization in ancient India, these renouncers were shaped by their world, but they also reshaped it—as teachers, preachers, and exemplars. They were the new intellectuals—carriers of cultural and linguistic changes; they were also wandering minstrels, keepers and transmitters of an oral culture. The changes and trends set into motion by the renouncers continued for several centuries during which Buddhism, especially when spreading into Central Asia, became both a transmuted entity and a transmutative influence.

Consistent with this broader movement, the Buddha's public activities after his awakening were predominantly urban, although he himself favored the life of the recluse.

> [The Buddha's] was a life spent in great urban and trading centers of the time where people came together to trade and to deliberate, to study and to practice their special crafts and industries, to discuss and to be entertained, to seek justice, to make money, or to find the truth. The appeal of his doctrines was primarily to men of an urban background. Among the things which, tradition suggests, might be said in praise of him was that he abstained from 'village ways,' *gama Dharma*, a term which could also be translated 'vile conduct.'...The point here seems to be that the Buddha's urbanity of speech was consistent with the rational quality of the ideas which he expressed.[8]

Here we find a paradox: On one hand, the Buddha encouraged his followers to abandon family ties and seek the wanderer's life in order to gain awakening, while, on the other hand, there were more householders than ordained monastics among his followers and friends. These included kings and princes, as well as merchants and professionals. Together this group represented a new urban civilization, spearheaded by prosperous merchants who placed a premium on new areas of learning—mathematics, astronomy, and etymology. The Brahmins, representing the old learning, concentrated on memorizing the myriad verses of the Vedas, but that was often was the extent of their knowledge. The new learning made it possible for merchants to expand their activities along international trade routes in the northwestern parts of the subcontinent. The Buddha's revolutionary contribution to the new learning was a language of rational presentation and psychological analysis, which appealed greatly to the urban intellectuals who were challenging the claims of the entrenched Brahminical teachings and power structures everywhere—in politics, society, and religion.

These new urban intellectuals may have eventually challenged similar claims made by arhats within orthodox Buddhist groups. The followers of the new learning may have been willing to support the arhats as religious successors to the historical Buddha, but not as sole interpreters of his teaching.

The phase that is now variously called primitive Buddhism, early Buddhism, Pali Buddhism, or Nikaya Buddhism lasted for about two hundred years after the death of the Buddha. I have primarily used the term Nikaya Buddhism in this commentary to denote this early period of Buddhist history. This label is not without its own sets of problems, but it is being increasingly used by scholars.

Nikaya Buddhism was an oral culture, and its setting was monastic. Tradition tells us that by the time of the Second Council, held in the city of Vaishali about a hundred years after the passing away of the Buddha, fissures had already appeared in the thinking of some in the monastic community who wanted a more liberal interpretation of the monastic rules.

The conflict between lay followers and monastics and disputes about what the true Dharma is and who knows it have been central features of Buddhist history since that time and have led to the formation of new schools in almost every generation in every Buddhist culture. The term *sasana* is perhaps the nearest ancient equivalent of the modern expression "Buddhism." (The term as an "ism" has been an attempt by European colonizers to understand a foreign tradition through their own religious and conceptual framework; many of the assumptions implicit in the European framework do not obtain in Buddhist history in Asia. This continues to be a subtle problem in our contemporary understanding of the tradition.)

> *Sasana,* [in its developed sense] denotes a system. It has a socio-religious content and is used as a term of delimitation, with a touch perhaps of communal consciousness too, "within the *Sasana*" meaning "within the Buddhist system of faith and its rule of living."[9]

The absence of any centralized authority within the sasana rendered irrelevant the question of conformity or nonconformity. The modern Theravada school of Sri Lanka, representing Nikaya Buddhism, has tried to establish itself in a position of authority by claiming that its canon is definitive. The Sthaviras, their ancestors in ancient India, championed the view that other schools of Buddhism were heterodox. "Sthavira" literally

means "elder" and denotes those monks who believed that the sutra collection in the Tripitaka was the one and only authoritative teaching of the
historical Buddha. But going back to the time of the Buddha himself, the
tradition had been extraordinarily tolerant of "free thinking" as in, for
example, the Buddha's advice to the Kalamas.[10] The added problems of
geographical isolation and linguistic diversity in pre-Ashoka Buddhism
only reinforced the tendency for independent thinking and interpretation
among non-Magadhan monks—those monks who had been venturing
westward and southward and were not in touch with the finer points of
monastic debates in and around Rajagraha, Shravasti, and Vaishali.

The schism at the Second Council led to the formation of the Mahasanghika sect, which became the dominant voice for ideas that would later
be collectively called Mahayana, even though it is possible to discern the
presence of these ideas in all the early schools, including the orthodox
ones. Historical records differ as to exactly what issues precipitated this
split, but a general consensus seems to be that the Mahasanghikas refused
to accept the sutras and the Vinaya as the final authority regarding the
Buddha's teaching. The Mahasanghikas were thus the first rebels, reform-
ists, or schism-makers (depending on who is writing history), and they
ushered in a new way of thinking that eventually coalesced several centuries later into what we today know as Mahayana. Like the eleven schools
of Sthavira or orthodox Buddhism, the Mahasanghikas also split, inev-
itably, into a number of subgroups over a period of time.

At the Third Council held at Pataliputra (the capital of the Magadhan
empire) in 250 B.C.E. under the aegis of King Ashoka, the primacy of the
Sthaviras was established, and the dissenters were excluded from the sangha. It is important to note that this exclusion was in no way comparable
to excommunication in the Catholic Church; it only meant that the doctrines of the dissenting monks were not accepted by King Ashoka and the
orthodox monks, but the dissenting monks were still free to preach without royal patronage. The dissenters spread out westward, most notably to
Mathura (near present-day New Delhi), Kashmir, and other parts of northwestern India, thus creating "western Buddhism" in contradistinction to
Magadha-based "eastern Buddhism."

The Mauryan spread of Buddhism, under the patronage of Ashoka in
the newly unified subcontinent under one imperial authority, glorified
and legitimized for the masses what had hitherto been championed by a
relatively small group in north-central India: new opportunities for par-
ticipating in the wanderers' holy life, regardless of sex, creed, or caste. It

was during this flowering of the Ashokan period that Buddhism truly became a religion of the people. But the seeds for elitism were always there; in later centuries, donations of land and buildings by wealthy patrons allowed for monks and nuns to be no longer in touch with the daily life of the villagers. They were no longer in the service of the many but in the service of an institution. By the time of Brahmin re-ascendancy under the imperial Guptas at the beginning of the fourth century, Buddhism was on an irreversible course toward being marginalized in the public life of India and confined largely to great monastic universities. That Buddhism survived outside India for so many centuries is in no small measure due to the fact that in the countries of north and southeast Asia it took roots as a religion of the populace.

This transformation of Buddha's sangha in India from a regional to a continental entity and from a minor sect to a recipient of imperial patronage had enormous implications for the monastic community. New pressures appeared that transformed the sangha despite itself, and in the process the whole timbre and resonance of Buddha's teachings were changed from their earliest presentations. The pre-Ashokan sangha had primarily consisted of renunciates, monks and nuns devoting their lives to the exclusive goal of *nirvana*. As a result of Ashoka's patronage, the transformed entity became a universal, international religion in which the interests of the laity became equally important.

Any mention of Mahayana within the context of this commentary must follow the caveat that the term Mahayana did not come into usage until several centuries after the initial split between the Sthaviras and the Mahasanghikas (the *Diamond Sutra*, for example, does not use the term at all). The Mahasanghika School remained the primary focus of new trends of thought that had moved away from the Sthavira model. The new movement called itself *Bodhisattvayana* to emphasize its conscious embracing of the path of the bodhisattva. Mahayana is not and never was a single, unitary phenomenon. It is not a sect or a school, but rather a spiritual movement, which initially gained its identity not by definition, but by distinguishing itself from alternative spiritual movements or tendencies then current; it was essentially a culmination of various earlier developments.

A lot of nonsense has been said and written about the Hinayana-Mahayana controversy. Well-intentioned but myopic people have been in the thick of this controversy. To a large extent, this controversy thrives on emotions generated by word choices. "Hina" means "lower" or "inferior" but it can also mean "humble" or "narrow." Depending on the context, "Hinayana" can mean the path that is "narrow and deep," and "Mahayana" can mean "wide and shallow."

The more aggressive users of the term "Mahayana" have been insensitive in making extravagant claims at the expense of followers of Nikaya Buddhism. At the heart of these distorted perceptions we find social, political, and economic issues, even issues of power and authority. In the politically correct, internationalized West, the term "Theravada" has replaced "Hinayana," which is not without its difficulties, but it works to defuse the traditional animosity between the followers of northern and southern branches of Buddhism.

In our own time and place, those not co-opted into the sectarianism of Asian settings are seeking creative ways to describe the reality of this earliest phase of the tradition. A contemporary scholar has suggested "Foundational Buddhism,"[11] which I think is a very apt description. I like to call the earliest layer "Psychological Buddhism," and the later phase, the so-called Mahayana, "Visionary Buddhism." These terms are not exclusive but manage to capture the basic orientation of each of the two phases. The use of the term "Psychological Buddhism" acknowledges the tremendous revolution Siddhartha Gautama brought about in the religious climate of his time, moving the debate from metaphysical speculations to the working of individual consciousness. It does not come as a surprise then that the contemporary Western intellectual and psychological tradition should discover great nuggets in Pali texts dealing with the Buddha's teachings on mind and its role in the shaping of bondage or awakening.

This argument sees Visionary Buddhism not as a rejection of Psychological Buddhism, but as a refocusing of elements that are strongly present in the enlightenment experience of the Buddha, though wisely not the main thrust of his teachings. For such an experience is beyond the grasp of ordinary human mind; the Buddha's enterprise, if anything, was to point out certain universal operative principles that Psychological Buddhism was most uniquely qualified to propagate.

A close reading of the available material shows that the Mahasanghika School was a reaction against the conservative tendencies within the nascent Buddhist religion in the second and first centuries B.C.E. Although the genesis of this reaction may be found as early as the Second Council, it was not an organized movement or a rejection of the strengths of Psychological Buddhism.

It is perhaps best to regard the Mahayana as a social movement of monks, nuns, and lay people that began in reaction against the controls exercised by a powerful monastic institution. This movement was responsible for the production and dissemination of a body of literature that challenged the authority of that institution by having the Buddha proclaim a superior and more inclusive path and a more profound wisdom. In subsequent centuries, during which sutras continued to be composed, the Mahayana became not merely a collection of cults of the book but a self-conscious scholastic entity. [12]

The divide between the laity and the religious specialists was never as sharp as has been made out by partisan scholars; monasticism continued to be a powerful force within Indian Mahayana throughout its tenure. What's more, the scholastic/analytic approach of the Abhidharmist monks did not define the totality of the Sthavira/Theravada monks whose cause it sought to champion. There were a number of good Theravada monks who did not know Abhidharma and were quite happy to be deprived of its technical structure. What seems most likely is that for nearly a millennium after the death of the Buddha the broad tradition based on his teachings was both an influencer and an influencee in a multicultural marketplace, so to speak, of competing religious and philosophical ideas that emerged in India after Alexander's invasion in 323 B.C.E.

A distinction needs to be made between the Abhidharmist monks and the mystically inspired persons on both sides of the divide. The Mahasanghikas had their own Abhidharma as did some other subschools of Sthavira. At the same time, the nascent Mahayana movement was driven by mystical and devotional paradigms, and the impulse of these followers was to reclaim the mystical inspiration of the Buddha. They figured there was more to contemplative life than lists, categories, and subcategories; often the devotional and the mystical aspects of the human heart are not satisfied by mere technical information. In that sense, the Mahasanghika followers were not that far apart from the non-Abhidharmist Theravada monks.

Even later, when the Madhyamaka philosophers of the Mahayana developed philosophical tools to respond to the Abhidharmist scholars, the debates were limited to an intellectual elite within the Buddhist community. A large majority of the community went about its own business, doing different practices in order to be inspired by the vision of awakening as outlined in Buddha's life and teachings. Many of these practices were influenced by what was happening in the larger society around them rather than the intra-Buddhist philosophical debates.

The momentous changes that were taking place within the Buddhist sangha in the years following the reign of King Ashoka were but a reflection of the political and societal turmoil going on around it. The Mauryan empire disintegrated rapidly after Ashoka's death, and the years between 200 B.C.E. and 300 C.E. were a time of bewildering political change in India. Yet beneath this confusion one thing provided continuity and cohesion—trade. The Mauryan empire had opened up the subcontinent by building roads and imposing a uniform system of administration. It created ideal conditions for merchants in the mid-Gangetic valley to open up trade routes with the Mediterranean world and China.

The newly prosperous mercantile community organized itself into guilds, which became important influences in urban life, both in the production and distribution of goods and in shaping public opinion. The emergence of guilds and international mercantile activity gave rise to a written culture with Sanskrit as an international language, a development that had tremendous impact on how the Buddhist sangha thought about itself and how it presented itself to those outside the fold.

The pre-Buddhist Vedic culture had been an oral tradition, although there is some evidence that written languages did exist at the time. A body of sacred texts transmitted orally from teacher to student (in most cases, from father to son) had allowed the Brahmin priests to maintain their hold on the religious and intellectual life of Indian society. In the two or three centuries following the death of the Buddha the vast oral canon of the Pali sutras had remained the province of monks who specialized in their memorization. But the oral process also promoted elitism within the sangha, which, coupled with the insistence of the Sthaviras that they alone were the true repository of the Buddha's teachings, gave rise to dissatisfaction among those monks who proposed that the Buddha had taught therapeutically rather than as a metaphysician. In their view, there was room for creative interpretation of the Buddha's teachings. The rise of written culture allowed dissenting monks to express important perceptual shifts within the tradition. The first of these was championed by the Mahasanghikas:

> The Mahasanghikas were in the course of time led to an increasing skepticism about the value of verbalized and conceptual

knowledge. Some of them taught that all worldly things are unreal, because [they are] a result of the perverted views. Only that which transcends worldly things and can be called "emptiness," being the absence of them all, is real. Others said that everything, both worldly and supramundane, both absolute and relative, both Samsara and Nirvana, is fictitious and unreal and that all we have got is a number of verbal expressions to which nothing real corresponds. In this way the Mahasanghikas early implanted the seeds which came to fruition in Mahayana.[13]

Mahayana, as a historical cultural process, contained a number of shifts that eventually led to the rise of philosophically important schools such as Madhyamaka and Yogachara and their subschools, as well as breakaway religious experiments like Zen and Tantra. Within India this process lasted for a thousand years or more after the death of the Buddha, and a number of shifts coalesced during this period that were eventually to influence the shape of Buddhism in east and north Asia. These shifts were not always discernible to those who were engaged in different experiments in their own time and place; there was no single person who experienced all these shifts in his or her lifetime. It is only with hindsight that we have created our own unique ways of looking at them:

Shift from a "developmental" model to "discovery" model: Although these are contemporary terms, we may speculate that the Mahasanghika followers felt that one of the problems of a map-oriented developmental model such as the Abhidharma is that of verification. In theory, it is possible to have a map and say that an arhat has completed the map and is therefore fully developed or liberated. However, to the Mahasanghikas, this self-proclaimed awakening did not conform to how the Buddha taught, for he did not lay out a map in the sense that the later masters of Abhidharma did. So long as the Buddha was alive he could be counted upon as a source of verification of attainment of arhatship in others. In the following centuries, as the production of arhats dwindled, the problem of verification became a contentious issue.

The Mahasanghika shift was thus *from the rigid, scholastic, and developmental map of the Abhidharmists to modalities of religious experimentation* where each person had the freedom to discover for him- or herself the perils and promise of the path.

Shift from the psychological to the mystical: An important aspect of the discovery model for early Mahayanists was the shift from the idea that mind can be a knowable, dynamic process to an exploration of the universe as a sacred mystery; of its ineffability. This was a *shift from analysis to transformation* in which the tendency of the analytic approach for elaboration or explanation was discarded in favor of experiential absorption and allowing the nonverbal experience to be transformational. Hence it was a *shift from the intellectual to the experiential* in which dissatisfaction with the rigidity of Abhidharma scholasticism led to an effort to recover the fresh intuition of the principles behind the doctrines.

Shift from scriptural codification to models of awakening: An inevitable result of the above shifts was the move away from affiliation with a fixed canon to the observation of examples set by living persons; from a codification of the mechanics of awakening to faith in an "enlightened" person as a model of awakening. This shift may have been influenced by the inspiring presence of saints, regardless of what they could teach and whether or not their understanding conformed to the Abhidharma model.

Such a change in perspective may have led to a *shift from debating fraternities to co-devotionalists.* It has been suggested that by the time of Ashoka, the so called "eighteen schools" of Buddhism (there may in fact have been as many as thirty) had in effect turned into debating fraternities; and the ascetic practices of the first generation of monks and nuns were no longer central to the life of these fraternities. The shift may have been a catalyst for inserting devotional, even mystical, fervor into a debating environment.

Another shift, perhaps an overarching one, may have been *from a monochromatic to a polymorphous culture.* The Buddhists of the second century B.C.E. in India may have been chafing at a debate-centered Abhidharma model, lacking in love and devotion. The need of the hour may have been for a language of the heart, of poetry, color.

The bodhisattva model opened up the possibility of a *shift from a parts mentality to a wholeness mentality.* One of the Mahasanghika criticisms of the arhat model was that it was self-centered. The bodhisattva model, working for the benefit of all sentient beings, was offered as an alternative. In fact, one of the central themes of developed Mahayana, as also of the *Diamond Sutra,* is the inseparability of one being from another. An offshoot of this shift may have been yet another *shift—from a commitment to individual healing to a commitment to communal healing.*

A major shift in early Mahayana was *a shift from obedience (to the Vinaya rules) to creativity in individual expression,* which brought about another, perhaps dubious, shift, several centuries later, *from the ascetic to the aes-*

thetic. In medieval Japan and China we see the culmination of this trend in the high visibility of Buddhist poetry and visual arts, at times to the detriment of meditational pursuits.

Perhaps the most decisive shift in the movement from Psychological Buddhism to Visionary Buddhism was the *shift from the historical to the transcendental* in terms of the changing status of the Buddha. For the Sthaviras, the Buddha Shakyamuni was a historical personage—a great teacher but not a divinity. The Mahayanists, however, saw the Buddha as a transcendental principle rather than a mere individual in the phenomenal world. Over time, this formulation led to an elaborate Mahayana cosmology, which posited buddha fields and the three bodies of the Buddha. In the popular imagination in the countries of north and east Asia, the notion of "living Buddhas" came to replace the historical Shakyamuni. This development was not without its cultural and sociological causes and consequences.

The *shift from an oral to a written culture* permitted the encapsulation of a number of trends that were already present in the incipient Mahasanghika dissent. As the center of political power moved away in the post-Ashokan period from Magadha to the northwestern parts of India, there was a corresponding shift from an eastern, Pali-based Buddhism to a western, Sanskrit-based Buddhism. The accompanying shift, *from the analytical approach of Pali Abhidharma to more poetic modes of expression in Sanskrit,* allowed the Mahayana followers to be more in touch with trends in secular literature of their time, which was, of course, in Sanskrit.

None of these shifts took place overnight or were even obvious at the time. But certainly the rise of written culture and the establishment of settled monasticism changed the character of the sangha as never before. The transition from a wandering mendicant to a settled monk, from a forest dweller to an urban temple administrator, meant an increasing dependence on wealthy lay followers for economic support. It was a recipe for some chaotic interactions, and not always auspicious for the future of the ordained sangha.

The transformations that have taken place within Mahayana may seem almost violent from the perspective of Nikaya Buddhism but, as Edward Conze has noted,

> Throughout its history, Buddhism has the unity of an organism, in that each new development takes place in continuity from the previous one. Nothing could look more different from

a tadpole than a frog and yet they are stages of the same animal, and evolve continuously from each other. The Buddhist capacity for metamorphosis must astound those who only see the end-products separated by long intervals of time, as different as chrysalis and butterfly. In fact they are connected by many gradations, which lead from one to the other and which only close study can detect. There is in Buddhism really no innovation, but what seems so is in fact a subtle adaptation of pre-existing ideas. Great attention has always been paid to continuous doctrinal development and to the proper transmission of the teaching. These are not the anarchic philosophizings of individualists who strive for originality at all costs.[14]

The Mahayana Sutras

IN THE TWO CENTURIES following the death of the Buddha certain monks systematized the teachings of the Buddha to present them as a more coherent whole. This effort led, in the following centuries, to the creation of lists and categories, a compendium of a systematic philosophy that became known as Abhidharma, which was added to the sutras and the Vinaya to become the last of the "Three Baskets" (Tripitaka).

The hallmark of Abhidharma literature was its conversion of the Buddha's teaching of no-self *(anatman)* into a rigid scholastic system. According to this principle, all events in the mind, body, and cosmos can be explained as a plurality of momentary phenomena or *dharmas* without reference to a permanent, abiding self. Abhidharma postulated that dharmas correspond to irreducible phenomena—both physical and mental—and are the basic building blocks of reality. Moreover, each of the dharmas has its own beingness *(svabhava),* which means that it can exist and function without need of a personal agent. These Abhidharma categories became a major catalyst for the emergence of Prajnaparamita literature including the *Diamond Sutra,* the earliest religious texts of what would become the Mahayana movement.

Parallel to doctrinal debates of the time, a Sanskrit literary genre called the Avadana, literally, "great deed," added a new layer of complexity and a push toward the rise of Mahayana. Avadana literature marks the transitional stage between Nikaya Buddhism and Mahayana sutras. This genre sets out three paths in the pursuit of awakening: (1) the path to arhatship, (2) the path to becoming a *pratyekabuddha* or solitary awakened one, and (3) the path of the bodhisattva in order to become a *samyaksambuddha* or fully awakened one. We will see an amplification of these terms in following pages, but it is noteworthy that in the Avadana literature all three paths are accorded respect.

This literature also introduced the notion of a buddha field, which was originally construed as the power of a Buddha to enable the seeds of generosity directed toward him to bear fruit. The stories in this genre also stress the importance of vows based on acts of merit—that a meritorious act will bear fruit in the direction of the vow. Another aspect of the genre consists of biographies and legends (found in the *Theragatha* and *Therigatha* section of the Khuddaka Nikaya) about the previous lives of early Buddhist monks and nuns. These were recited by monks to lay believers in later generations and share a basic structure: a monk or a nun states that in a previous life he or she met such-and-such a Buddha, performed various virtuous deeds, experienced happiness in heaven and on earth, and was finally reborn into the time of Shakyamuni Buddha in order undertake the final journey into nirvana. The purpose of these discourses was to impress upon listeners the causal relationship in which good deeds bring about good results, and bad deeds, bad results, and to produce a blueprint for awakening in the new universal society championed by King Ashoka. This universalism honored the participation of women in the life of the new sangha in some significant ways.

A contemporary historian of the Avadana literature says that in this genre

> we can see more than soteriology at work; different biographies incorporate and inscribe new calculations of time, new geographies and cosmologies, new forms of political activity. The moral biographies of the nuns, including "Gotami's Story," addresses, further, certain problems that had emerged concerning the role of women in Buddhist practice. On the one hand, the nuns provided paradigmatic counterparts to the monks; without them one-half of universal society, the female half, would have been excluded from the new revelation of universal soteriology. On the other hand, the nuns' stories, which were most likely composed by women, unmistakably combat misogynist attitudes that continued among Indian Buddhists despite the Buddha's own apparent egalitarianism.[15]

Through establishing a causal relationship between virtuous deeds, vows, and good rebirth, the Avadana literature set the stage for the Mahayanists to paint their own picture of the spiritual path, with the premise that only the bodhisattva path is valid.

The hallmark of the flowering Mahayana movement was its sutra literature rather than any one doctrine or practice. Some of the earliest Mahayana sutras were perhaps composed orally, while others were written down.

While the authenticity of the Pali sutras is accepted by all Buddhists, it did not prevent the preachers of ancient Buddhism from "embellishing the kernel of a Dharma-theme with their own innovations."

> About 100 B.C.E. a number of Buddhists felt that the existing statements of the doctrine had become stale and useless. In the conviction that the Dharma requires ever new re-formulations so as to meet the needs of new ages, new populations and new social circumstances, they set out to produce a new literature. The creation of this literature is one of the most magnificent outbursts of creative energy known to human history and it was sustained for about four to five centuries.[16]

The texts of Nikaya Buddhism were a closed system; any scholarship in this area was commentarial, confined wholly to analysis or synthesis of the rules and doctrine. Speculative philosophy was not, to say the least, their forte. The Mahayana texts, on the other hand, were extra-traditional (from the Nikaya perspective) and baroque. It is important to remember that the Mahayana sutras were seen by their adherents in the earliest phase of development as revelatory scriptures, not philosophical tracts. The philosophical/commentarial tradition associated with these sutras developed many centuries later, primarily at the great medieval Buddhist universities of Nalanda, Vikramashila, and elsewhere. A contemporary scholar has captured the spirit and essence of the Mahayana sutras in these words:

> The great Mahayana sutras form the center of Mahayana; in them the new religious inspiration is crystallized. A massive and imposing body of literature, the sutras differ greatly in content, but each and every one of them breathes the spirit of Mahayana. These widely scattered writings serve many religious communities. While individual sutras or groups of sutras take up particular themes, they concur and overlap at many points. Moreover, one and the same sutra can give rise to different religious movements. They are often accompanied by explanatory commentaries, or sastras. Nearly all the sutras and sastras of Mahayana Buddhism are written in Sanskrit, which means that they originated in Indian Buddhism. Translated into Chinese and Tibetan, these texts had a much more extensive influence in East Asia than in their Indian motherland.[17]

The origin of Mahayana sutras is a matter of enduring controversy. Followers claimed, and still claim, that the words were spoken directly by the Buddha himself. Most Mahayana believers in east and north Asia have no awareness of Pali sutras as the earliest body of Buddhist literature. They believe that the Mahayana sutras, with which they are familiar in a limited fashion, are the original teachings of the Buddha.

The Mahayana argument that its sutras are the mystical inspiration of the Buddha and contain his messianic teachings takes the view that a lot of material was edited out of the sutra collection in the Pali canon. In some cases this may be true and worth further examination. However, the secondary Mahayana argument is clearly self-serving: that their sutras needed to be kept secret for five hundred years because the developing societies after the Buddha's death needed time for preparation and purification through the monastic education and societal ethics he had taught in the Pali canon.

The only thing that can be said with any degree of certainty is that the development of the Mahayana tradition and literature was not the product of an organized or unitary movement. It was initially, perhaps, nothing more than a perceptual shift within Buddhism where many people insisted on seeing the Buddha Shakyamuni as something more than a historical figure. Mahayana also sought a new model of religious aspiration in that it advocated and glorified the path of the bodhisattva, the aspiration to full buddhahood for the welfare of others, and saw itself as a path available to anyone, whether monk or lay person.

This perceptual shift is not just an academic issue. Buddhologists in this century are dealing with the problem of what is and what is not a legitimate text. The status of Buddha Shakyamuni, which began to change almost immediately after his death, is central to this debate. The Mahayana innovation was to see the Buddha as an archetype, a *nirmanakaya* or projected form of a universal principle. The proliferation of hundreds of practice schools in east Asia in later centuries meant that each school had a founder, who was regarded by most of the followers of that school as a Buddha and whose (mostly) oral teachings were enshrined as sacred texts. Within the insular environment of each school, these texts replaced the texts of the early canons altogether, and, in most cases, replaced even the great Mahayana sutras of Indian origin.

This trend lies also at the heart of modern charismatic Buddhist movements in east Asia in this century, especially Japan and Korea. The connection of these movements to historical Buddhism is often quite tangential. In most cases, the founder was not even familiar with the teachings of

Shakyamuni Buddha, but called him- or herself a Buddhist simply because he or she was born in a Buddhist family and culture. The challenge for contemporary Buddhology is to determine which methodological approach to take in evaluating these founders, their sermons, and writings.

This challenge is present also in any investigation of the development of Mahayana sutras in ancient India, but there the historical importance of the emerging genre of sutra literature remains undiminished. The Mahayana sutras, written in Sanskrit rather than Pali or early Prakrit dialects, ushered in an era of what may be called Sanskrit Buddhism, which in turn became a bridge to Sanskrit-based classical Hinduism. Independent of the rise of Mahayana, by the beginning of the Christian era Sanskrit had become the language of international culture in Asia. At the time of the early Mahayana sutras, Sanskrit or some form of Sanskrit vernacular had displaced Pali and early Prakrit dialects as the language of study in Buddhism in India. Sanskrit Buddhism took root in northwestern India and spread to Central Asia and eventually to China. But it also spread into eastern and southern India and made an impact on the linguistic orientation of the Buddhism of the time. Sarvastivadins, who belonged to one of the earliest and most influential schools of Nikaya Buddhism, flourished in northwestern India. They included a number of prominent scholars in their ranks and compiled their commentaries in classical Sanskrit.

The eighteen schools of Buddhism that flourished at the time of King Ashoka were distinguished by geographic location and doctrinal interpretation by individual monks. These commentarial differences, in turn, gave rise to the composition of Abhidharma literature where the doctrine was codified once and for all. But this codification, in turn, produced a backlash and gave rise to the composition of Mahayana sutras.

The production of sutras in northwestern India and Central Asia is still a matter of continuing scholarly investigation.

> Some sutras appeared first in Prakrit or in the languages of Central Asia (e.g., Tocharian and Uighur), but by the sixth century, when the sutras were studied at the university at Nalanda, they had been rewritten in Sanskrit (with some lingering traces of Prakrit colloquialism). It was the adoption of Sanskrit as the official language of the Gupta dynasty in 320 C.E. that caused the shift from Prakrit. Nearly all the inscriptions on pre-Gupta monuments and tablets are in Prakrit, but almost all similar inscriptions made after the founding of the Gupta dynasty are in Sanskrit.[18]

The composition of the Mahayana sutras spanned a creative period of roughly five hundred years from 100 B.C.E. to 400 C.E. A secondary stage of production continued well into the eighth century. There are no first-hand historical sources on the origins of this literary movement, but a number of sociocultural factors that gave rise to the movement can be discerned from the sutras themselves.

It seems almost certain that the earliest strata of Mahayana sutras was the work of visionaries and inspired believers; in some form or the other this trend has continued throughout Mahayana history, and thus it may not be too much of a stretch to call it Visionary Buddhism. Given the gradual but far-reaching shift from an oral to a written culture, and given the tendency of ancient Indian society to venerate sacred literature, it is not surprising that over a period of several hundred years innovative trends within the Mahayana sutra literature employed increasingly dramatic metaphors and images to establish itself. Just as in our own time, computers and the internet are redefining our sense of how we think about ourselves and the world around us, so did the emergence of a written culture influence the Buddhists of ancient India in how they saw themselves and the world around them. The Mahayana sutra literature gave a distinct flavor and tone to these new ways of thinking.

> The landscape of the Mahayana sutras is quite extraordinary, space and time expand and conflate, connections seem to be missed, we move abruptly from ideas so compressed and arcane as to verge on the meaningless, to page after page of repetition …Sometimes stories or sermons which must have originally circulated separately, products, perhaps, of a different intellectual milieu, are inserted into the text. It is occasionally possible to detect short insertions by comparison of the prose and the verse version of a particular episode, for many of the sutras have both. Generally the verses are older. The metric form prevents easy tampering, and it is possible sometimes to detect archaic or non-standard linguistic features which indicate, together with other clues, that a number of the early Mahayana sutras were not originally in Sanskrit at all, but in a Middle Indic dialect which has been subsequently Sanskritized—not always well from a classical point of view.[19]

As a general characterization, Mahayana sutras are a poetry of religious faith, a far cry from the dry analyses and categories of the Abhidharma. The exuberance of the Mahayanists seems at odds with the austere practices and minimalist doctrines of Nikaya Buddhism and may have been a celebration of an environment of intellectual freedom within the new written culture where they found themselves free to reinterpret the traditional teachings creatively in their own words. The rise of written culture naturally allowed greater freedom for elaboration. Thus, if at times we detect an evangelical fervor in some of these sutras, it is perhaps understandable in light of the intellectual and religious dynamics spurring the new movement.

Lama Anagarika Govinda argues that the continuation of this impulse was the singlemost significant factor responsible for the rejuvenation of Buddhism in the various cultures of Asia in different generations through the creation of new typologies of religious vocation:

> It was the protest of the Siddhas of India, the mystics and sages of Tibet, the Ch'an patriarchs of China and the Zen Masters of Japan, that rejuvenated the religious life of Buddhism and freed it from the shackles of mediocrity and routine and widened its scope beyond the confines of an exclusively monastic ideal...[20]

As has been argued above, the earliest Mahasanghika followers were religious aspirants, pure and simple, seeking a new form of wisdom. Theirs was the way of devotion and faith, not of mere academic intellectualism for its own sake. They were inspired, it seems, by the visionary aspects of their practice and its fruit—the aspiration to become a perfected Buddha.

As distinct from the commonly respected body of canonical texts of Nikaya Buddhism, the Prajnaparamita approach within early Mahayana was centered on the worship of a number of books as revelatory texts rather than on *stupa* worship, which was the most common kind of devotional practice in the pre-Prajnaparamita period. Groups of followers, both monks and lay people, studied and worshipped particular sutras. This tendency became even more pronounced later on in Chinese Buddhism, whence it spread to the rest of north Asia. In today's Japan, for instance, we find powerful Buddhist sects following the teachings of the *Lotus Sutra* sometimes to the exclusion of the rest of the Buddhist tradition. Many Mahayana sutras conclude with the declaration that immense merit can be obtained from studying, memorizing, or just worshipping even one verse of that particular sutra. On the other end of the evangelical spectrum, some sutras denounce those who denigrate or oppose their teachings; only these teachings, the sutras insist, will lead to final emancipation.

The authorship of the Mahayana sutras, like the origins of the Mahayana movement, is a matter of continued conjecture. Contemporary historian Paul Williams argues that these sutras were a product of monks' efforts:

> We have no names of lay people who contributed to the doctrinal origins of the Mahayana. The Mahayana sutras were clearly the products of monks, albeit monks whose vision of the Dharma embraced the aspirations of the laity, and who used lay figures in the sutras to embody a critique of other monks seen as elitist or perhaps ultra-conservative.[21]

In support of his argument he cites the *Pratyutpanna Sutra,* which states that in the future one group of monks will accuse another group of monks of having fabricated the sutra:

> We see how literary sources support the epigraphic evidence that early Mahayana was very much a monastic movement with little widespread support.[22]

He cites another sutra, the *Ajitasena Sutra,* to highlight what he calls the "Mahayana before Mahayana." He argues that there was a proto-Mahayana stage prior to Mahayana's self-awareness as Mahayana, "with all the concomitant senses of superiority and contrast with religious practices and beliefs deemed inferior."[23]

Talking specifically of the *Ajitasena Sutra,* Williams further states,

> The text ends in the traditional manner of early Mahayana sutras. Those who promulgate this sutra will attain Buddhahood, while those who listen to even one verse will become bodhisattvas. The preachers of Dharma who recite this sutra will receive favorable rebirths and ultimately become enlightened. Those who condemn the sutra will go to some very nasty hells. …what marks this sutra is the supremacy of Buddhahood and the possibility of anyone, monk or lay, becoming a bodhisattva.[24]

The Prajnaparamita Sutras

B UDDHIST SCHOLARSHIP generally agrees that the Prajnaparamita sutras represent the earliest layer of Mahayana sutra literature. Conze has distinguished four phases of development:

1. 100 B.C.E. to 100 C.E. This period is characterized by the formation and composition of the basic text. The oldest text from this period is the *Ashtasahasrika* or the *Prajnaparamita in Eight Thousand Verses*.
2. 100 C.E. to 300 C.E. In this period the basic texts are expanded. The *Shatasahasrika Sutra* (100,000 verses), the *Panchavimshatisahasrika Sutra* (25,000 verses), and the *Ashtadashasahasrika Sutra* (18,000 verses) belong to this period.
3. 300 C.E. to 500 C.E. This period is characterized by the restatement of the basic ideas in short sutras on the one hand and versified summaries on the other. The *Vajrachedika Prajnaparamita Sutra* (the *Diamond Sutra,* also know as the *Prajnaparamita in Three Hundred Verses*) and the *Hridaya Prajnaparamita Sutra (Heart Sutra)* belong to this period.
4. 500 C.E. to 1200 C.E. This period is characterized by the influence of the tantras, evidence of magical elements in the sutras and their usage. An example from this period is the *Adhyardhashatika Prajnaparamita Sutra* (150 verses).

In positing the Prajnaparamita sutras as the foundation stone of the Mahayana edifice, a contemporary scholar has noted:

> These perfect wisdom texts served as the foundation for a sys-
> tematic curriculum developed over many centuries in the
> Mahayana Buddhist monastic universities, among the earliest
> universities on this planet. This curriculum involved three
> phases. There was first a phase of memorization of the basic

> Prajnaparamita texts, as well as of the systematic updated in-
> terpretations that made the text live anew for succeeding gen-
> erations...[25]

As the name of the cumulative literature indicates, these sutras focus on the perfection of wisdom and are thus called the "wisdom sutras." The perfection of wisdom in these sutras is the development of insight into *shunyata*, the empty nature or the purely relative existence of all dharmas, the realization that things of the world have relative existence and derive their validity solely from a nexus of causal conditions. In their relative existence they exist in their suchness, and any reification of their existence as real, in and of itself, is imposed on them by linguistic and conceptual categories. It is this reification, produced by ignorance *(avidya),* that is the central concern of the wisdom sutras.

A theme parallel to suchness and shunyata in the Prajnaparamita sutras is karuna (compassion). It is a long-standing paradox in the Buddhist tradition: if all existence is *shunya* or insubstantial, to what or to whom is compassion directed? This paradox has been one of the creative impulses in the Buddhist philosophical and practice traditions. For the practitioner, the understanding of wisdom and compassion—and the inherent tension between the two—is not to be resolved on a theoretical level, but to be experienced in one's own mind and body. In this way one finds emptiness and compassion to be mutually supportive rather than mutually contradictory.

The Western philosophical tradition took a decisive turn with the advent of Aristotelian logic, which insisted that a paradox could not exist without movement toward reconciliation. The Hegelian dialectic became its most vocal champion in modern times, occupying the position that the presence of a "thesis" instantly gives rise to an "antithesis" and the incompatibility of the two must lead to a "synthesis," which in turn becomes another thesis, giving rise to another antithesis, and so on ad infinitum.

In Asian philosophical and religious traditions, on the other hand, paradox has been embraced joyfully, even willfully, perhaps because the Asian intellectual tradition has always seen life itself to be paradoxical. Nowhere is the embracing of paradox so joyful as in the Prajnaparamita-Madhyamaka tradition, which later gave rise to Ch'an (Zen) in China. The koan method of the Zen tradition has become one of the most celebratory hymns to the creative use of paradox. The Zen use of the koan as a translogical position has always baffled the logical, linear mind.

The *Diamond Sutra,* as arguably the most important Mahayana wis-

dom text to prefigure the Zen tradition, has its share of paradoxical sayings. Perhaps none is more baffling than Buddha's words "saving all beings
knowing full well that there is no one to save."

Subsequent "systematic updated interpretations" within the Mahayana
gave rise to the philosophical schools of Madhyamaka and Yogachara in
India. Each of these three phases of Indian Mahayana—Prajnaparamita,
Madhyamaka, and Yogachara—has played a complementarily influential
role in the emergence of numerous schools of Buddhism in China, Korea,
Japan, and Tibet. The Prajnaparamita is largely a devotional approach,
while Madhyamaka is primarily philosophical, providing scholastic theses and debating tools to substantiate the insights of the Prajnaparamita.
The early Yogachara is a philosophic offshoot of Madhyamaka, adding to
the repertoire of philosophical notions of Madhyamaka. The later Yogachara is a more existentially experimental approach to completing the task
first begun in Prajnaparamita.

These three elements of Indian Mahayana remain influential to this day
as foundation stones wherever Mahayana Buddhism is practiced. By necessity, there is an overlap whenever one discusses the major themes of Mahayana for each theme is embedded in all three phases and is not the exclusive
domain of any. Discussion of any Mahayana theme necessarily references a
developmental process covering several centuries of practice and reflection.

A Thematic Understanding
of the Prajnaparamita Tradition

THIS SECTION is intended to provide an in-depth discussion of the basic architecture of Mahayana themes as they are understood within the Prajnaparamita tradition. Some readers may choose to skip this section in their first reading and come back to it later for greater clarification.

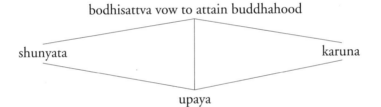

The **bodhisattva vow** provides the context and the inspiration to motivate the individual to gain insight into **shunyata** (emptiness), the essential nature of all phenomena, which leads to an experience of *tathata* (of suchness), of things as they are in their essential nature, of the mutual identity of phenomenal and transcendent reality. At the same time they cultivate **karuna** (compassion) for all those still caught in delusions, and help them through **upaya** (skillful means) so that they too may become free and attain buddhahood.

This is what we may call a psychological or existential template, free of the metaphysical or cosmological underpinnings of Mahayana. It may be restated as follows:

Intention: to gain awakening for oneself
  and to help all beings attain awakening
Cognition: shunyata
Experience: [of] karuna and tathata
Engagement: upaya

While this existential model may be helpful in limited ways, almost all of Mahayana rests on a cosmological perspective in which the spiritual journey of the bodhisattva begins with: (1) meeting a fully enlightened Buddha and being inspired or awakened by him or her to the point of an arousal of *bodhichitta*, the thought of awakening, and (2) taking the bodhisattva vow in order to eventually become a Buddha to help all sentient beings arouse their own bodhichitta and follow the path of buddhahood. This process may last for hundreds of lifetimes, but there is an unshakable faith that with the perfection of the *paramitas* (perfections) it will eventually lead to buddhahood.

In some Mahayana subcultures like the Vajrayana, the arousal of bodhichitta is considered an irreversible process; some schools of Vajrayana postulate bodhichitta as a particle-like, granular substance that gathers within itself the fruits of practice and becomes the repository of the potentiality of buddhahood. In the Pure Land variation, the attainment of buddhahood includes the creation of buddha fields *(buddhakshetra)* into which all supplicants will be reborn. (See a fuller discussion of these terms on pages 103–8.)

Along the path, the bodhisattva gains insight into the nature of the phenomenal world, which is found to be lacking *(shunya)* in "own-being" *(svabhava)*. This insight is ineffable wisdom *(prajna)*. It is awakening *(nirvana);* it also allows the bodhisattva to see the mutual identity of *samsara* (the phenomenal world and its delusions) and nirvana (the transcendent, which is understood only in relation to the phenomenal), that is, as bipolar aspects of the same reality rather than as two exclusive realities.

As a result of this insight, the bodhisattva cultivates compassion for those beings who are still caught in the delusions of the phenomenal world. Compassion is both a causal factor, as part of the original vow, and a fruit of cultivation for the bodhisattva. In the cultivation of compassion, the bodhisattva is motivated by a wish for the awakening of all beings because he or she has seen the utter inseparability of him- or herself from the rest of the universe. This is the notion of suchness *(tathata).* The inseparability of oneself from others and the intention to guide others to awakening are also seen through the wisdom of shunyata through which the bodhisattva clings to nothing and is not invested in anything.

From within a state of wisdom the bodhisattva perceives all beings as empty, as no-things on the absolute level, while seeing the suffering of oneself and others on the relative level. Motivated by compassion for oneself and others, the bodhisattva strives to bring the wisdom of shunyata to one and all. The liberating technique the bodhisattva introduces to help others is skillful means *(upaya),* and he or she engages in skillful means knowing full well that teachings themselves can be nothing more than skillful means.

The journey of a bodhisattva is thus emblematic of a fusion of wisdom and compassion. The greatness of the bodhisattva is that—despite insight into the emptiness of the phenomenal world—he or she does not withdraw from it. Instead, he or she engages in samsara solely within the framework of skillful means. If authentic, all the activities of the bodhisattva are skillful means expressing wisdom and compassion.

Within the context of this commentary on the *Diamond Sutra,* I have found it useful to examine three interlinked core Mahayana themes—skillful means, wisdom, and compassion, and the bodhisattva path—to bring into a single braid, as it were, the explication of the sutra.

SKILLFUL MEANS

The concept of upaya or skillful means appears not only as the central working proposition of the *Diamond Sutra* but also as the core organizing principle of the Mahayana. While the theme of the bodhisattva path serves as preparatory background in the sutra, the real focus is on upaya whose function is to bridge the seeming incompatibility of emptiness and compassion. Indeed, emptiness and compassion themselves may be regarded as skillful means. Upaya is one of the perfections *(paramitas)* cultivated by the bodhisattva and is associated with the seventh of the ten stages *(bhumi)* of development on the path to buddhahood.

A view common to all schools of Buddhism is that the Buddha's approach to teaching was primarily therapeutic—that he used a variety of strategies in assessment of the abilities of his audience to bring his listeners to a realization of nirvana. A commonly quoted saying of the Buddha is that the knowledge he gained through his awakening experience could be compared to the leaves in a forest; by contrast, the teachings he imparted to his listeners were a mere handful of leaves. He had chosen, he said, to teach only those points that would help his listeners attain higher knowledge and dispassion in the service of awakening and cessation of suffering.[26]

The Mahayanists elaborated this idea further to propose that all the teachings and practices were provisional and were established by the Buddha for the benefit of the unenlightened. They claimed that skillful means are infinite, while the early schools maintained that only the eightfold path was skillful. The Mahayana premise is that as a practitioner continues on his or her path, he or she easily recognizes the provisional quality of the teachings and does not become delusionally attached to them. The task of the bodhisattva is to use these provisional teachings as skillful means to facilitate the passage of all beings toward nirvana.

Although the term skillful means occurs only rarely in the Pali canon, one comes away from the reading of Pali sutras with a sense that the Buddha saw his Dharma teachings as skillful means and not as an end in itself; right views or the eightfold path were part of the path to the goal, but could not express the goal itself. The most famous simile to describe the teachings as upaya has been that of the raft: If a person comes to a river he wishes to cross but finds it swollen with heavy monsoon rains, he could collect grass, twigs, branches, and leaves and bind them together to build a raft in order to cross safely to the far shore. But he would be foolish if he were to get attached to the raft and try to carry it on his shoulder when he went inland. The raft has served it purpose; the best thing he can do is haul it up onto the river bank for others to use or set it adrift in the water, and then go on.

> So I have shown you how the Dharma is similar to a raft, being for the purpose of crossing over, not for the purpose of grasping. Bhikshus, when you know the Dharma to be similar to a raft, you should abandon even good states, how much more so bad states.[27]

This directive—cautioning us ultimately to abandon the "good" states as well as the "bad"—is perhaps one of the most remarkable statements in religious history. Of course, one abandons the raft only *after* crossing the river, not while crossing it. Similarly, one abandons concern for the notion of good or bad states only after one is grounded in direct realization. A fundamental difference in the interpretation of the raft simile is that in Nikaya understanding, one abandons concern with good and bad *after* one gets to where one wants to go; the Mahayana understanding, in some schools, is that one abandons concern with good and bad *in order* to get to where one wants to go. These differences in interpretation may be one area where more creative responses emerge as Buddhist teachings are reflected upon in the West.

Upaya is synonymous with the view that sees all of Buddha's teachings as an antidote to suffering rather than as an ideology. Establishing this view is the sole enterprise of the *Diamond Sutra.*

The later Zen tradition enthusiastically took up this call for abandonment of all views. The following verse from the Korean Zen tradition captures the spirit of Buddha's admonition:

> Good and evil have no self nature;
> Holy and unholy are empty names;
> In front of the door is the land of stillness and quiet;
> Spring comes, grass grows by itself.[28]

Closely related to the idea of the Dharma as a raft is the notion of a wise person as a skillful boatman who, knowing the Dharma, ferries others across a dangerous river. Samsara is synonymous with the currents of greed, hatred, and delusion in a swiftly flowing river in which those who do not understand the Dharma are swept away, unable to help themselves or others. The wise teacher is:

> As one who boards a sturdy boat,
> With oars and rudder well equipt,
> May many others then help across,
> Sure, skillful knower of the means.[29]

The assertion that the Buddha's teaching was therapeutically directed toward awakening and was not itself to be grasped became the cornerstone of the new movement within Buddhism. The early Mahayanists understood the self-transcending function of right view. They saw the basic teachings such as the noble eightfold path as skillful means and not as doctrine. For them it was a right view *(samyak drishti)* in the service of awakening as a skillful means but nothing more. The Abhidharmist insistence on rigidifying Buddha's teachings as entities in and of themselves alarmed early Mahayanists who responded by writing sutras of their own that celebrate the ability of a bodhisattva to guide beings to awakening through skillful means.

The Abhidharma movement arose in the first place as a response to the inconsistencies found in the Pali sutras but soon became rigidified into a self-sustaining system. The Mahayanists, on the other hand, embraced the inconsistencies and proposed that the Buddha's teachings have relative value and relative truth. When used properly, as a skillful means, such a teaching transcends itself. The value of approaching the teachings of the Buddha as relative, as therapeutic rather than absolute, lies in the fact that it allows one to see all the contradictions and inconsistencies as only apparent. Teachings are appropriate to the context in which they are given; their truth is relative, and contradictions evaporate. This is a non-dogmatic approach to truth where one investigates one's own experience with complete honesty.

The concept of upaya became crucial to the historical development of the Mahayana impulse. Guided by the conviction that the mere wish to help all living beings would not by itself be effective without insight into viable and effective methods, the dedicated monks accompanying international trade caravans in western India and central Asia modified their own rules of conduct (Vinaya) so as to make themselves more acceptable to local cultures and ways of thinking. In this way, upaya became an ideal tool for missionary monks in their propagation of the Dharma within and outside the borders of India. We must also note that not all monks going west and north amended the rules; orthodox and non-orthodox monks disagreed on whether there was one set of skillful means (the eightfold path) or many. The history of how these differences played out at the grass roots level in central Asian Buddhism, to take one example, remains largely unknown to us today.

In east Asia especially the concept of upaya gained unprecedented importance. The *Lotus Sutra*, perhaps the most influential of the Mahayana sutras in east Asia, is a paean to the concept of upaya. We find in the *Lotus Sutra* a parable of a burning house, which is perhaps the best known upaya parable in the Mahayana sutras. It uses the hypothetical situation of an immensely wealthy father in a fabulous mansion with many rooms in which his many children are playing, each one fascinated with his or her own toys. Suddenly the house catches on fire and is in imminent danger of burning to the ground with the children still inside engrossed with their toys. The wise father, seeing the danger, calls out to each one by name and promises each a cartload of toys of his or her particular fancy. In this way he gets all the children safely out of the burning house. Here the Buddha is compared to the wise father, or the wise physician, who understands the individual sickness of each of his disciples and prescribes a different medicine for each one, even though the prescriptions may seem contradictory. To Buddha prescriptions such as these are skillful means to get suffering beings out of the realm of samsara, not rigid religious formulas to which disciples must adhere.

It may not be an exaggeration to say that Mahayana is a history of upaya in search of Buddhas. The path of buddhahood is concerned with discerning infinite skillful means for the welfare of others. A feeling for upaya, rather than concern with monastic minutiae, gave Mahayana a practical emphasis on evaluating and finding redress for suffering in the world. It found inspiration in stories like that of Kisa Gotami and the mustard seed[30] from the earlier layer of the tradition and took that example as its primary modality. The Mahayana tradition contains many upaya parables that are contrary to the spirit and letter of the Vinaya of the Nikaya and other pre-Mahayana traditions. The flexibility of Mahayana ethics allows it to see everything in the phenomenal world, including itself, as relative and provisional.

Conze has this to say about upaya:

> "Skill in means" is the ability to bring out the spiritual potentialities of different people, by statements or actions which are adjusted to their needs and adapted to their capacity for comprehension. If the truth be told, all that we have described so far as constituting the doctrine of the Mahayana is just "skill in means" and nothing more. It is a series of fictions elaborated to further the salvation of beings. In actual fact there are no Buddhas, no Bodhisattvas, no perfections, and no stages. All these are products of our imagination, just expedients, concessions to the needs of ignorant people, designed to ferry them across to the Beyond. Everything apart from the One, also called "Emptiness" or "Suchness," is devoid of real existence, and whatever may be said about it is ultimately untrue, false and nugatory. But nevertheless it is not only permissible, but even useful to say it, because the salvation of beings demands it.[31]

For the Mahayanists, the skillful means approach resolved the inherent tension between wisdom and compassion since, in an absolute sense, wisdom according to Mahayana sees everything as empty of own-being—there are no beings and no suffering; there is no awakening and nothing to be liberated from. The rarefied air of this wisdom is indeed hard to breathe. However, on the relative level, Mahayana sees deluded beings caught in illusory suffering. This is the modality to which the efforts of the bodhisattva are directed. The Mahayana formulation, as expressed in the famous line from the *Heart Sutra* "Form does not differ from emptiness; emptiness does not differ from form," postulates that only the relative realm of suffering can be directly apprehended by the senses. Because deluded engagement in the relative realm is the only data of experience for most human beings, the bodhisattva is motivated to act in compassionate ways to help them see the transcendent dimension of their experience. Thus compassion and wisdom are the substance or ground of skillful means, and skillful means are the function of compassion and wisdom.

In the best expressions of Mahayana, both emptiness and compassion are teachings that are skillful means; each should be used in its appropriate sphere and then left behind when going beyond that sphere. This is the sense in which the doctrine of skillful means underlies everything in the Mahayana tradition. The motive of compassion and skillful means, accompanied by a grounding in wisdom, became an overriding concern for the new Mahayana thinkers in medieval India.

This new way of thinking offered itself as an alternative to scholastic Buddhism in eastern India in the pre-Ashoka period and as a religion fit for export in western India in the post-Ashokan centuries. The rallying slogan for the transformed religion was a Buddha doesn't teach a rigid philosophical system for its own sake—he teaches it out of compassion for the suffering of beings; all teachings are tailored to the circumstances and capacities of those for whom they are intended. Even though Mahayana always remained a minority movement in eastern India, and even though Nikaya Buddhism was also exported to Central Asia and China in the early centuries, the upaya-based forms of Mahayana became totally dominant in China and elsewhere in east Asia in later centuries.

Such emphasis on skillful means is always a risky engagement. One edits one's motives considerably as one makes sense of the activity in which one is engaged, and in an unenlightened mind this can often take the form of psychological misplacement of motives and emotions. The working proposition in Mahayana is that a perfected Buddha apprehends the causal connections of past, present, and future both in him- or herself and in others and is able to see simultaneously the myriad interconnecting patterns of existence, both individual and collective. Thus the skillful means suggested by him or her in a given situation come out of a purified and unhindered consciousness. This premise also accepts that whatever mistakes one makes as a bodhisattva, the unshakable quality of bodhichitta remains unchanged, and the bodhisattva takes complete karmic responsibility for his or her mistakes and misadventures.

SHUNYATA

Translating the Sanskrit word shunyata into Western languages has always been problematic. When translated as "voidness" or "emptiness," it has a nihilistic undertone, which is how the orientalists of the nineteenth century saw and portrayed Buddhism. Fortunately our understanding of the term and of Buddhism itself has grown in recent decades and has prevailed over the earlier misinterpretations.

The root of the word comes from the verb *svi,* meaning "to swell." The Buddhist usage of this verb in the compound term shunyata is to indicate the true nature of a swelling or a bubble, which appears to be an enclosure but is in reality hollow or contentless. In the Buddhist wisdom tradition, its usage is a tool with which to distinguish between appearance and reality. When one is deluded, one assumes that what is apprehended by the senses (that is, the bubble) contains something identifiable or graspable; the corrective application of prajna wisdom allows one to see that all appearances are illusory, with nothing inherent to grasp. This prajna wisdom does not automatically invalidate appearances, but challenges us to investigate the nature of reality more closely.

Shunyata (Pali: *sunnata*) appears in the Pali canon, but was generally ignored by the Abhidharma systematizers. In the Pali sutras, this term is used in a twofold sense. First, it refers to a direct mode of perception in which nothing is added to or subtracted from the actual data perceived. This modality of perception perceives a thought as a thought, for example, irrespective of the contents of the thought and without attending to the question of whether or not there is a thinker. When this modality of perception apprehends something in a visual field, it perceives the object as an experience of seeing rather than as an affirmation or denial of the existence of the object behind the experience. The same notion applies to each sense organ and its function. In this modality, nirvana is considered to be the highest form of shunyata in the present life—the uncorrupted mode of awareness of things as they are. In the second sense, shunyata refers to the lack of a selfhood (that is, anything incapable of self-identification) in the six senses and their objects. In other words, shunyata is both a mode of perception and an attribute of things perceived.[32]

The Abhidharmists maintained that even though an individual person is empty of self, there are dharmas that have their "own-being" (svabhava) and are the building blocks of the universe. Early Mahayana thinkers attacked this notion and accused the Abhidharmists of being attached to a subtle notion of "self" in the dharmas, of being substantialists, and thus incapable of truly understanding the Buddha's teachings. Mahayana thought was supported by parallel developments in the science of mathematics in India at that time.

> In the fourth century B.C.E., the linguist Panini had developed the concept of zero (Sanskrit, shunya) to symbolize empty but functioning positions in his analysis of Sanskrit grammar. (He proposed that every word was composed of a root and a suffix, so words without suffixes actually had the zero suffix.) Mathematicians eventually borrowed the concept to supply an essential principle of the decimal notation we use today: that a place in a system may be empty (like the zeros in 10,000) but can still function in relationship to the rest of the system.[33]

The central doctrinal controversy between the Abhidharmists and the early Mahayana thinkers thus rested on the former's assertion that the irreducible dharmas forming the ultimate building blocks of experience were each endowed with svabhava, their own particular being or nature. The Mahayanists posited that all dharmas were empty of svabhava. Even though conditional relations (between two dharmas) functioned as interdependent co-arisings,

> ...there were no "essences" acting as nodes in the relationships, just as mathematical relationships could function among the integers in the decimal notation even if they were only zeroes. In fact, if dharmas had any essence, the principles of causation and the Four Noble Truths could not operate, for essences by nature cannot change, and thus cannot be subject to causal conditions. Whether the Abhidharmists meant the concept of svabhava to imply an unchanging essence is a moot point, but in time the doctrine of emptiness became a rallying point for the rejection of the entire Abhidharma enterprise.[34]

One way to understand the controversy between the Abhidharmists and the early Mahayana thinkers is through the parallel developments in physics between the Newtonian atomic theory, which corresponds to the Abhidharma position, and quantum subatomic theory, which corresponds to the Mahayana position.

In my commentary on the *Heart Sutra* I attempted to point out how the findings of quantum physics have added a new dimension to our understanding of the term shunyata and what it stands for. Here are some excerpts from that commentary as they bear on a discussion of shunyata:

> For a very long time, the Newtonian/Cartesian scientific view of the world rested on the notion of solid, indestructible particles as the building blocks of matter and all life, moving in space and influencing each other by forces of gravitation and interacting according to fixed and unchangeable laws. This myth disintegrated under the impact of experimental and theoretical evidence produced by quantum physicists in the early decades of this century. The experiments of quantum physics showed that the atoms, the presumed fundamental building blocks of the universe, were, at their core, essentially empty. In experiments, subatomic particles showed the same paradoxical nature as light, manifesting either as particles or waves depending on how the experiment was set up.
>
> Quantum physics has thus brought about a radical new understanding both of the particles and the void. In subatomic physics, mass is no longer seen as a material substance but is recognized as a form of energy. When a piece of seemingly solid matter—a rock or a human hand or the limb of a tree—is placed under a powerful electronic microscope:
>
>> the electron-scanning microscope, with the power to magnify several thousand times, takes us down into a realm that has the look of the sea about it. In the kingdom of the corpuscles, there is transfiguration and there is samsara, the endless round of birth and death. Every passing second, some 2½ million red cells are born; every second, the same number die. The typical cell lives about 110 days, then becomes tired and decrepit. There are no lingering deaths here, for when a cell loses its vital force, it somehow attracts the attention of macrophage.
>>
>> As the magnification increases, the flesh does begin to dissolve. Muscle fiber now takes on a fully crystalline aspect. We can see that it is made of long, spiral

molecules in orderly array. And all of these molecules are swaying like wheat in the wind, connected with one another and held in place by invisible waves that pulse many trillions of times a second.

What are the molecules made of? As we move closer, we see atoms, the tiny shadowy balls dancing around their fixed locations in the molecules, sometimes changing position with their partners in perfect rhythms. And now we focus on one of the atoms; its interior is lightly veiled by a cloud of electrons. We come closer, increasing the magnification. The shell dissolves and we look…inside to find…nothing.

Somewhere within that emptiness, we know is a nucleus. We scan the space, and there it is, a tiny dot. At last, we have discovered something hard and solid, a reference point. But no! As we move closer to the nucleus, it too begins to dissolve. It too is nothing more than an oscillating field, waves of rhythm. Inside the nucleus are other organized fields: protons, neutrons, even smaller "particles." Each of these, upon our approach, also dissolve into pure rhythm.

These days they (the scientists) are looking for quarks, strange subatomic entities, having qualities which they describe with such words as upness, downness, charm, strangeness, truth, beauty, color, and flavor. But no matter. If we could get close enough to these wondrous quarks, they too would melt away. They too would have to give up all pretense of solidity. Even their speed and relationship would be unclear, leaving them only relationship and pattern of vibration.

Of what is the body made? It is made of emptiness and rhythm. At the ultimate heart of the body, at the heart of the world, there is no solidity. Once again, there is only the dance.

[At] the unimaginable heart of the atom, the compact nucleus, we have found no solid object, but rather a dynamic pattern of tightly confined energy vibrating perhaps 1022 times a second: a dance. The

protons—the positively charged knots in the pattern
of the nucleus—are not only powerful; they are very
old. Along with the much lighter electrons that spin
and vibrate around the outer regions of the atom, the
protons constitute the most ancient entities of matter in the universe, going back to the first seconds
after the birth of space and time.[35]

It follows then that in the world of subatomic physics there are
no objects, only processes. Atoms consist of particles and these
particles are not made of any solid material substance. When
we observe them under a microscope, we never see any substance; we rather observe dynamic patterns, continually changing into one another—a continuous dance of energy. This
dance of energy, the underlying rhythm of the universe, is again
more intuited than seen. Jack Kornfield, a contemporary teacher
of meditation, finds a parallel between the behavior of subatomic particles and meditational states:

When the mind becomes very silent, you can clearly see
that all that exists in the world are brief moments of consciousness arising together with the six sense objects. There
is only sight and the knowing of sight, sound and the
knowing of sound, smell, taste and the knowing of them,
thoughts and the knowing of thoughts. If you can make
the mind very focused, as you can in meditation, you see
that the whole breaks down into these small events of sight
and the knowing, sound and the knowing, and thought
and the knowing. No longer are these houses, cars, bodies, or even oneself. All you see are particles of consciousness as experience. Yet you can go deep in meditation in
another way and the mind becomes very still. You will see
differently that consciousness is like waves, like a sea, an
ocean. Now it is not particles but instead every sight and
sound is contained in this ocean of consciousness. From
this perspective, there is no sense of particles at all.[36]

Energy, whether of wave or particle, is associated with activity,
with dynamic change. Thus the core of the universe—whether

we see it as the heart of the atom or our own consciousness—
is not static but in a state of constant and dynamic change. This
energy—now wave, now particle—infuses each and every form
at the cellular level. No form exists without being infused by
this universal energy; form and energy interpenetrate each other
endlessly in an ever-changing dance of the molecules, creating
our universe. This universal energy is itself a process, beyond
the confines of time and space; a form, on the other hand, is an
"event," existing momentarily in time and space. This "moment"
may last for seventy or eighty years in the case of a human being,
a thousand years in the case of a sequoia tree, a few million years
in the case of a mountain, but internally, at the cellular level,
each of these forms is in a process of change at any given
moment. In the paradigms of quantum physics, there is ceaseless change at the core of the universe; in the paradigm of Mahayana wisdom, there too is ceaseless change at the core of our
consciousness and of the universe.[37]

The new paradigm in quantum physics is a replacement of atomism/
reductionism with the dynamic qualities of web relationships. It a replacement of the Cartesian/Newtonian formulation of an objective world "out
there," which can be investigated independent of the investigator, with an
interconnected, "ecological" model in which the investigator is not separated from the object of investigation and whose "being" affects the quality of investigation as much as the object itself. This paradigm of quantum
physics parallels the Mahayana wisdom (prajnaparamita) of ancient India
that sees each and every form as a compounded entity, created and held
in place momentarily by a number of conditioning factors coming together. Because it is compounded, it has no core independent of the conditioning factors that are responsible for its creation. Hence it is empty of
an own-being (svabhava) or self-essence (svabhavata); it is rather made up
of a web of relationships, which are dynamic in character and interconnected in complex ways in which the observer and the observed share
equally the responsibility for the momentary appearance of phenomena.
  David Bohm, one of the leading physicists of this century, sees the tangible reality of our everyday lives as a kind of illusion—a holographic
image. In his work, Bohm postulates two orders of reality: the manifest-
ed is the "explicate" or the "unfolded" order while the deeper level is the

"implicate" or the "enfolded" order. The universe is a result of countless "enfoldings" and "unfoldings" between these two orders:

> …electrons and all other particles are no more substantive or permanent than the form a geyser of water takes as it gushes out of a fountain. They are sustained by the constant flux from the implicate order, and when a particle appears to be destroyed, it is not lost. It has merely enfolded back into the deeper order from which it sprang.
>
> The constant and flowing exchange between the two orders explains how particles, such as the electron in the postironium atom, can shapeshift from one kind of particle to another. Such shiftings can be viewed as one particle, say an electron, enfolding back into the implicate order while another, a photon, unfolds and takes its place. It also explains how a quantum can manifest as either a particle or a wave.[38]

In a model paralleling a geyser of water gushing out of a fountain, the later Mahayana-Yogachara teachings posit that the five *skandhas* (conglomerations—of materiality, feelings, perceptions, mental formations, and consciousness) are constantly arising out of shunyata or *dharmakaya* (the body of truth).

The Yogachara formulations of shunyata in the later Mahayana sought to "improve" the purely dialectical approach of the earlier Madhyamaka. Here shunyata is equated with dharmakaya and used in the sense of "ground of being," similar to the implicate order in quantum physics proposed by David Bohm. When each of the skandhas has run its course, it enfolds back into shunyata. In their transitory and momentary appearance they are constantly interacting with one another, and each interaction produces a *bija* (seed or imprint). This imprint is what enfolds back into shunyata or dharmakaya. In Yogachara, both shunyata and dharmakaya are synonymous with *tathagatagarbha*, the "womb of the Tathagata," which refers to a cosmic consciousness as the repository of individual and collective karmic seeds, but which in itself remains unstained by such seeds.

Naturally, Bohm does not address the issue of imprints resulting from mutual interactions of the implicate and the explicate orders, which is the domain of Buddhist perspectives on karma and rebirth. In Yogachara formulations of *alayavijnana,* the "storehouse consciousness," there is the notion of "seeds" (that result from an encounter of the six senses with the phenomenal world) falling into the storehouse consciousness, which is akin to our subconscious mind. How these seeds interact with "old" seeds already present in the storehouse consciousness and "new" seeds that might be coming in even as a particular seed is finding its "locality" in the storehouse consciousness is a matter of great psychological research. There is currently a great deal of interest in the psychological understandings of the Buddhist tradition, and both traditions are the richer for it.

The Bohmian interplay of the implicate and the explicate orders may be viewed by Buddhist thinkers as the interplay of the absolute and the relative. At the implicate level, there is an incredible amount of energy, which is the same energy that produces streaking comets, burning stars, and scattering radiation in the cosmos. The explicate order is a manifestation of that energy, but it collapses back into the underlying implicate order. The energy at the implicate level is absolute for it is indivisible; its manifestation in the world of forms (as in a geyser) is the realm of the relative, and the absolute and the relative are in a dynamic, interdependent relationship. Theoretically, the absolute need not be in an interdependent relationship, but in our experience as human beings we do not encounter the absolute as a stand-alone absolute; we encounter it through the relative.

In order to protect us from becoming fixated on the notion of the absolute as a stand-alone entity, the Madhyamaka thinkers in early Mahayana advanced the "two truths theory," which helped bridge the apparent gap between emptiness and compassion by accepting the relative, qualified truth of the realm of appearances. Nirvana and samsara are seen as conflation or synergetic loops as in the Bohmian model. Thus the relative truth of the experience of *dukkha* (unsatisfactoriness) could be accepted, and a compassionate perspective brought to it without compromising the ultimate or absolute truth of emptiness. In the best sense of the term, the Yogacharins saw their own formulation as another upaya, rather than as an ideology to be defended.

Modern physics sees the speed of light as the absolute; time and space are relative. The absolute and mysterious nature of the speed of light forms a bridge between the relative, objective world we see around us to the infinite realm beyond time and space. Physicists now describe all matter as frozen light. Paradoxically, this frozen light is also dynamic movement and the cause of incalculable enfoldings and unfoldings between the two orders.

The existence of a deeper and holographically organized order also explains why reality becomes nonlocal at the subquantum level. Because everything in the cosmos is made out of the seamless holographic fabric of the implicate order, it is meaningless to view the universe as composed of parts, as it is to view the different geysers in a fountain as separate from the water out of which they flow. Despite the apparent separability of things at the explicate level, everything is a seamless extension of everything else, and ultimately even the implicate and the explicate orders blend into each other.[39]

While quantum physics sees the two orders as energy configurations blending into each other, ultimately becoming inseparable, the Mahayana thinkers saw the mutual identity and inseparability of samsara and nirvana—"Form does not differ from emptiness, emptiness does not differ from form"—as a way of being in the world, free from rigid ideologies and willing to help all beings in the process of liberation. This is the path of the bodhisattva on the way to buddhahood.

COMPASSION AND THE BODHISATTVA PATH

The theme of compassion was embedded in the Buddhist tradition right from the very beginning and forms the core organizing principle of Shakyamuni Buddha's teaching career. Various accounts of the Buddha's enlightenment all agree that after the momentous event, when he was ambivalent as to whether or not to share with others what he himself had experienced, it was compassion for all beings that finally motivated him to teach.

In the Pali sutras, compassion is included as one aspect of the fourfold *brahmavihara* ("divine abodes" or "joyful states") schema. But Nikaya Buddhism was by and large geared more toward the attainment of nirvana for the individual. Compassion and the other brahmaviharas (loving-kindness, sympathetic joy, and equanimity) did not receive prominence until the later Mahayana tradition. Here again the central issue in this development is the shift from the ideal of the arhat to that of the perfected Buddha. An arhat-to-be rejects the world and all its quagmires; the bodhisattva as a Buddha-to-be chooses to function in the world, approaching the world's ills with compassion and seeking skillful means to redress them.

The Mahayana did not reject the wisdom approach of the Nikayas but sought to balance it with compassion. The result was a simultaneous practice of wisdom and compassion, which was seen as two wings of a bird—

a bird can not fly with one wing alone. Later iconographical depictions portray this balance by having Manjushri, the bodhisattva of wisdom, and Avalokiteshvara, the bodhisattva of compassion, flank Shakyamuni Buddha. In the countries of east Asia, compassion came to be seen as the primary quality of a bodhisattva, partly as a result of Pure Land developments.

The term bodhisattva and its usage are crucial in the development of Mahayana Buddhism, so much so that in the earliest stages of growth the Mahayana movement was known as *Bodhisattvayana* (the Bodhisattva Vehicle). Many of the Mahayana sutras are celebratory hymns to the endeavors of the bodhisattva. The *Diamond Sutra*, like most Mahayana sutras, elaborates upon the virtues of the bodhisattva.

The path of the bodhisattva was seen by its proponents as quite different from the earlier paths of the arhat and the pratyekabuddha. The Mahayana innovation was to put emphasis on the bodhisattva path to the exclusion of the other two. But this emphasis has to be viewed in the light of Conze's thesis that there is no really new innovation in Buddhist intellectual history—every "new" idea is, in fact, a reworking of an idea already present somewhere in the tradition. Thus, in Nikaya Buddhism, we have the notion of the bodhisattva working his or her way toward appearing in the human world as Shakyamuni Buddha. This was the earliest notion of the bodhisattva—as the Buddha-to-be.

In the earliest stages of Buddhist history, the spiritual attainment of Siddhartha Gautama was viewed as essentially similar to those of his arhat disciples. Gradually, however, a vastly altered understanding of the former's attainment came into being as a result of the initial thrust of the embryonic Mahayana movement. The finer details of this alteration are not always easy to detect, but it seems safe to conjecture that this development was embedded in the accounts of the prior birth stories of the Buddha found in the Jataka narratives. Further elaborations of the bodhisattva idea were woven into the Jataka narrative structure and led to the Mahayana thesis that the attainment of perfect buddhahood as achieved by Shakyamuni Buddha was essentially superior to the attainment of the arhat.

In this elaboration, the destiny to become Buddha Shakyamuni began with a vow to attain perfect enlightenment made by the young monk Sumedha in the presence of another Buddha, Dipankara, many eons ago. This vow was confirmed when Dipankara Buddha made a prophecy that at such-and-such a time and place the young monk would attain buddhahood in our world system. In between these two events, during countless rebirths, the future Buddha labored as a bodhisattva to perfect himself in a variety of virtues or perfections. In contrast to this arduous path over many eons, the path of the sravakas or those who merely heard the Buddha preach was held by the Mahayanists to culminate not in buddhahood, but in the attainment of arhatship.

> Unlike a Buddha, an arhat comes to the Dharma through hearing it preached by others; he does not participate in the cosmic drama that results in the appearance of a Buddha in the world.[40]

The first schism in Buddhist history was between the Sthaviras and the Mahasanghikas and was rooted largely in a critique of the arhat ideal. This led to a displacement of the path of Sravakayana by the Bodhisattvayana.

What, then, we may ask, is a bodhisattva in Mahayana understanding? The word itself is a composite of two words: *bodhi + sattva. Bodhi* is derived from the Sanskrit verbal root *budh,* which means "to know" or "to be awakened." The word *sattva* has a wider range of meanings; in one sense it means "a being"; hence a bodhisattva is a being headed for awakening. This is the sense in which the term is understood in early Buddhism. A second meaning of sattva is "mind" *(citta)* or "intention" *(abhipraya).* In this sense, a bodhisattva is one who cultivates bodhichitta (wisdom mind) directed toward awakening. A third meaning of sattva is "strength" or "courage." In this sense the bodhisattva is one whose entire effort is directed toward awakening.

In the Pali canon, the term bodhisattva is used to identify Siddhartha Gautama before he became the Buddha. An implicit assumption in early Buddhism is that this term is to be used as a designation only for future historical Buddhas prior to their attainment of buddhahood. By contrast, Mahayana seized upon the concept of the bodhisattva as one of its most important spiritual ideals.

In the newly emerging Mahayana, the term bodhisattva was given a radical, new interpretation—it applies to anyone aspiring to buddhahood. According to a contemporary scholar of Buddhism,

> Motivated by extreme compassion (karuna), and tempered by the perfection of wisdom (prajna), the bodhisattva first completes three basic prerequisites that include generating the thought of awakening (bodhichitta), undertaking a formal vow to gain complete, perfect awakening for the sake of all sentient beings (pranidhana), and receiving a prediction with regard to

future attainment (vyakarna). Then, a path known as the bodhi-sattva path, and including ten stages (bhumis), is traversed. This path requires…deliberate rebirth in the cycle of samsara, and a sharing of all merit accrued with other sentient beings.[41]

As noted earlier, the shramana movement in India from the eighth century B.C.E. to the sixth century C.E. was a dynamic and continuous source of religious and cultural transformation. We can see how a new movement based on the bodhisattva ideal may have had a significant impact on the culture for it allowed the shramanas to be less exclusive. A minority of monks aligned with a larger number of lay practitioners may have felt, rightly or wrongly, that the monastic culture of Nikaya Buddhism was quite limited in fulfilling such an aspiration.

The Mahayana bodhisattva doctrine, a logical development from the older Buddhism but influenced by a complex set of factors, populated the heavens with forces of goodness, and presented Buddhism with a new mythology. As seen earlier, the new movement prospered greatly in the northwestern part of India where it was open to many influences from the Persian (the cult of Mithra, to take one example), the Middle Eastern, and the Mediterranean religions. Not the least of these influences on the development of Mahayana was the parallel rise of the *bhakti* (devotional) movement in a resurgent Hinduism.

In pre-Mahayana Buddhism, the Jataka stories, which were popular by the time of King Ashoka's reign, and accounts of the lives of the previous Buddhas were seen as purely descriptive and as tools for inspiring confidence in the teachings of Shakyamuni Buddha. In the new Mahayana movement, however, the training of the bodhisattva became prescriptive and was capped by a series of training steps. Proponents claimed that this new system of training was a substitute for, or even superior to, the eightfold path of the earlier classification.

In later Mahayana tradition, Indo-Tibetan scholars translated bodhisattva as *jangchub sempa* ("awakening mind hero"). This was an articulation of the bodhisattva as a new type of spiritual hero whose goal was quite different from that of the arhats or pratyekabuddhas. This bodhisattva aspired to nothing less than perfect buddhahood in order to access, as it were, unlimited upaya for helping those in distress. Early Mahayana saw the life of Shakyamuni Buddha as a paradigm of the inseparability of wisdom and compassion. This view argued that after realization, the Buddha chose to teach in this world out of compassion for all beings. The fact that about two hundred years after his death the monastic culture of his followers had become elitist and exclusive may have persuaded the Mahayanists that the monastics' concern for other beings was limited.

On all counts, the path of the bodhisattva became a core doctrinal innovation in the emerging Mahayana movement. It incorporated elements that were already present in the eightfold path of Nikaya Buddhism but in a different order and with some additions. The attainment of bodhisattvahood was much more difficult than arhatship and required greater commitment. This progression on the path of bodhisattvahood eventually came to be described as consisting of ten stages known as bhumis:

1. *Pramuditabhumi:* This is the state of joy that comes from arousing the thought of awakening (bodhichitta) and having taken the vow to become a perfected Buddha. This stage is characterized by the cultivation of giving *(danaparamita),* freedom from egotistical thoughts, and recognition of the emptiness of the ego and all dharmas. Thus a glimpse of prajnaparamita, the wisdom of emptiness, underscores even the first stage.

2. *Vimalabhumi:* This is the stage of purity where the bodhisattva perfects ethical conduct *(shilaparamita)* and through the practice of meditation *(dhyana)* is able to see and worship the heavenly Buddhas.

3. *Prabhakaribhumi:* This is the stage of radiance where the bodhisattva gains insight into impermanence and practices the perfection of patience *(kshanti paramita),* along with meditations on loving-kindness and compassion. He or she develops great forbearance in the face of adversity, masters anger, and is dedicated to exploring the depths of Dharma. Here the bodhisattva is said to have mastered the four *dhyanas* (states of absorption) and the four stages of formlessness and acquired the first five of the six supernatural powers.

4. *Archismatibhumi:* This is the stage of burning away the remaining wrong views where the bodhisattva develops the perfection of vigor *(viryaparamita)* and perfects the thirty-seven requisites of awakening required of a monk or nun.

5. *Sudurjayabhumi:* Literally "the land extremely difficult to conquer," this is where the bodhisattva further refines the thirty-seven requisites of awakening.

6. *Abhimukhibhumi:* This is the stage of wisdom where the bodhisattva gains insight into dependent co-arising *(pratityasamutpada)* and shunyata.

7. *Durangamabhumi:* Literally "the far-reaching land," this is where the

bodhisattva has gained thorough knowledge of skillful means, which enables him or her to lead any being on the way to awakening in accordance with that being's abilities. This stage denotes freedom from being reborn according to karma and becoming a "great being" *(mahasattva)* who can manifest him- or herself in any conceivable form in order to help and teach other beings. It is impossible for the bodhisattva to fall back into lower levels of existence after this stage.

8. *Achalabhumi:* This is the stage of immovability or non-relapsing where the bodhisattva is now certain to attain buddhahood. The bodhisattva can no longer be disturbed by anything because he or she has gained knowledge of when and where in the universe she can manifest at will. This stage is characterized by the ability to transfer merit to others and the cessation of further accumulation of karmic merits.

9. *Adhumatibhumi:* This is the stage of good thoughts where the wisdom of the bodhisattva is complete. He or she possesses all the supernatural powers as well as the teachings leading to awakening. This stage corresponds to the manifestation of Shakyamuni Buddha in this world.

10. *Dharmameghabhumi:* This is the stage of Dharma clouds, also known as *abhishekabhumi,* or the stage of coronation. This is where the dharmakaya of the bodhisattva is fully developed. He or she sits on a lotus in a heaven known as Tushita surrounded by countless bodhisattvas, and his or her buddhahood is confirmed by all the Buddhas. Bodhisattvas of this stage include Maitreya and Manjushri.

The new model allowed the followers of the bodhisattva path to focus on certain qualities of spiritual attainment rather than on a puritanical, monastic way of life. New texts were composed that touched upon ethical conduct more generally, without sharp distinctions between an ordained person and a lay practitioner. These texts, combined with others that address themselves to various Mahayana practices, see an ethical life as rooted in wisdom, compassion, and skillful means rather than in monastic strictures. Some of the bodhisattvas still chose to live the monastic life and abided by traditional monastic rules. In east Asian Buddhism a general sense of more relaxed rules of monastic conduct, sometimes loosely called the Mahayana Vinaya, emerged. These modified rules were a prescription for an ethical life without reference to the monastic judicial apparatus. The guiding vision for these modifications saw the Dharma as the cure for specific spiritual illnesses, a stance, its proponents claimed, that was in keeping with the appearance of Shakyamuni Buddha in this world as a physician for the spiritual illnesses of the world.

Maitreya, the future Buddha, is mentioned only once, and rather casually, in the Pali canon in the *Cakkavattisihanada Sutra* of the Digha Nikaya. It became logical that if there were Buddhas before Shakyamuni (the *Mahapadana Sutra* of the Digha Nikaya mentions a number of past Buddhas), there would be Buddhas after him as well. By the time of Kanishka (circa 100–200 C.E.), a cult of Maitreya was well entrenched in northwestern India. The notion of past Buddhas was most likely accepted even during the lifetime of Shakyamuni, and there is evidence that it was accepted by King Ashoka. By first century C.E., statues of future Buddhas appeared and the notion of past and future Buddhas seems to have been well established. We can only speculate what influence the concept of a world savior to come *(sayosant),* from the Persian religion of Zoroastrianism, might have exercised on these developments. Sayosant is the savior who, at the end of the world, would lead the forces of good and light against the forces of evil and darkness. Certainly there are enough similarities between the sayosant and the goal of the bodhisattva path to warrant investigation.

The bodhisattva was thought to embody not only a spirit of compassion but also one of voluntary suffering. At times, the resolve of the bodhisattva was expressed in almost Christian terms. The idea of the suffering savior may have existed in some form in the Middle East before Christianity arose, but it did not appear in Buddhism until after the beginning of the Christian era. The suffering bodhisattva so closely resembles the Christian conception of God in the form of Jesus who gave his life for others that we cannot dismiss the possibility that Buddhism borrowed this doctrine from Christianity, which was vigorous in Persia from the third century C.E. onward.

The Jataka stories show that bodhisattvas can be incarnated as human beings or even as animals, but the more advanced bodhisattvas, who have the greatest power for good, are divine beings in the heavens. Though neither omniscient nor almighty, the divine bodhisattvas can be beseeched and prayed to, for it is part of their mission to answer prayers. Thus the Bodhisattvayana opened two possible paths for a Mahayana believer: (1) perfecting oneself in the ten stages of bodhisattvahood, and (2) beseeching a perfected Buddha for protection and guidance.

The mahasattvas, as noted above, are the seventh-stage bodhisattvas who become celestial bodhisattvas. The compounded term therefore indicates the presence of both earthly and celestial bodhisattvas. Just as the bhikshu-sangha was a melange of newly ordained and highly attained aspirants, bodhisattvas were also classified in the Mahayana texts in terms of a mixture of different aspirations and persuasions. The levels of bodhisattva are listed below:

1. The newly embarked bodhisattvas who have not heard or who have rejected or will reject the perfection of wisdom, or shunyata
2. Bodhisattvas who have already set out for a long time but who have not heard or who have rejected or will reject the perfection of wisdom
3. Newly embarked bodhisattvas who hear and accept the perfection of wisdom
4. Bodhisattvas who have already set out for a long time and who hear and accept the perfection of wisdom
5. Irreversible bodhisattvas who will no longer backslide; these are the seventh-stage bodhisattvas, also called the mahasattvas
6. Irreversible bodhisattvas who have received knowledge (prediction) of where they will be reborn as celestial bodhisattvas to continue their work
7. Celestial bodhisattvas who work in different buddha fields to help all beings, such as Manjushri and Avalokiteshvara
8. Samyaksambuddha, a perfected Buddha, or Tathagata, such as Shakyamuni Buddha, who consciously chooses to be reborn into the human world to help teach others
9. Samyaksambuddhas who have become the dharmakaya and are no longer manifest in the world, such as Shakyamuni Buddha after his *parinirvana*

In the *Diamond Sutra* the Buddha speaks as a bodhisattva of the eighth category, a Samyaksambuddha who is in the world but not of it. He is rooted in the wisdom of shunyata but is motivated by compassion. He uses the language of the world to deconstruct the world so that a wisdom-based way of looking at things may emerge as skillful means. This wisdom is not formulaic and cannot be captured in words, for it has gone beyond words to a place where direct realization rather than conceptual verbalization is the essential mode of being.

The *Diamond Sutra* in the Mahayana

IN THE SPRING OF 1907 Marc Aurel Stein (later Sir Aurel), a British archeologist, stumbled upon the rock-hewn temple complex of the "caves of the thousand Buddhas" outside Dunhuang in the deserts of Gansu Province in the central Asian regions of China. Earlier he had gathered information in the walled town of Dunhuang that confirmed reports of the Hungarian explorer, Professor L. de Loczy, who had visited the district in 1879, concerning the existence of these caves, the walls of which were said to be covered with Buddhist frescoes and rock sculpture. These caves, sealed about the beginning of the millennium out of fear of invading nomads, yielded, for Stein and subsequent European collectors, an astonishing cache of some fifteen thousand Buddhist manuscripts, all on paper. There were also 1,130 paper bundles tied up with ribbon, many of which contained a dozen or more scrolls. In addition, there were numerous murals and wall paintings.

For nearly a thousand years, until the sealing of its cave-temples, Dunhuang had been an important way station on the Silk Road, playing host to the intrepid and the priestly, the two often being one and the same. Surrounded by bleak desert, its caves offered shelter and succor to travelers from the heat. Dunhuang had been an equally important center for the diffusion of Buddhism across central Asia and into China. The Buddhist monk, traveling east with merchant caravans from the northwestern parts of India, brought with him a new religious civilization that had been transforming the city-states along the southern and the northern routes of the Silk Road since the time of King Ashoka in the third century B.C.E. The Chinese merchant, traveling west from the ancient capitals of Loyang and Chang-an, brought with him his family values steeped in Confucianism and the empire of the Han. The two met in Dunhuang, and their meeting changed China.

The arid heat of the desert and the dark, cool interiors of the caves pre-served the paper manuscripts and paintings in almost pristine condition for some nine hundred years until the Stein discovery. Books from other regions were also in the caves, including Old Testament scriptures in Hebrew. Making secret arrangements with the Taoist priest in charge of the temple complex, Stein smuggled out twenty-nine packing cases con-taining manuscripts and paintings—enough to fill a museum—which were then sent to the British Museum in London. A year later, the French explorer M. Pelliot smuggled out an equally large booty, which was even-tually deposited at Libraire Nationale in Paris. Stein's and Pelliot's discov-eries captured the world's attention and transformed conventional Buddhist scholarship both inside and outside China. To this day, Stein and Pelliot are among those reviled by the Chinese as foreigners who robbed them of the bones of their history.

Among the manuscripts discovered in the Dunhuang caves was a copy of the *Diamond Sutra*, which was printed from a series of woodblocks, each reproducing an unalterable image of an entire page. The sheets were glued side-to-side and rolled into a scroll sixteen feet long. The title page shows a serene Buddha on a lotus throne guarded by angels and lions. The colophon says it was completed on the equivalent of May 11, 868 C.E., making it the world's oldest printed book, dated some seven hundred years before Gutenberg's invention of the printing press.

Long before the Dunhuang discovery, the *Diamond Sutra* had been one of the most revered texts of east Asian Buddhism. It is one of the prima-ry texts of the Prajnaparamita literature, which forms the earliest layer of the emerging Mahayana tradition in India, beginning around 100 B.C.E. Although the most commonly accepted date for the *Diamond Sutra* is around 350 C.E., it is possible that it is even older. Hajime Nakamura con-tends that the *Diamond Sutra* (and the *Heart Sutra*) should be dated to between 150 and 200 C.E.[42]

A relatively short text, the *Diamond Sutra* consists of thirty-two short chapters presenting a dialogue between the Buddha and his disciple Sub-huti, centered primarily on the twin themes of emptiness and the path of the bodhisattva. It enumerates the six perfections of the bodhisattva path but focuses on the perfection of wisdom.

Through the discussion of these two themes, the *Diamond Sutra* occu-pies a leading position in both a historical sense (the emergence of early Mahayana in the form of Bodhisattvayana) and a doctrinal sense (shun-yata as the central theme of the Prajnaparamita sutras, of which the *Dia-*

mond Sutra is an independent part). As mentioned earlier, as a system of thought, Buddhism is essentially paradoxical: the Abhidharma formulation of anatman (lack of a continuous self) sits uneasily with the notions of nirvana (awakening), karma, and rebirth. This tension is an inescapable part of the changes in doctrine and practices that culminate in the emergence of Mahayana. A historical and doctrinal understanding of the *Diamond Sutra*, therefore, requires an understanding of the larger Mahayana movement within Indian Buddhism between the first and fifth centuries, which formed the basis of central Asian, Chinese, Korean, Japanese, and Tibetan expressions of Buddhism in the centuries to follow.

The Role of the *Diamond Sutra* in the Zen Tradition

THROUGHOUT A LONG HISTORY of encounters with indigenous religious cultures, different schools of Buddhism developed a great variety of methods and approaches in response to specific historical, cultural, and geographical needs. In medieval India, in an age of great scholastic activity, there was the school of Madhyamaka philosophy for the intellectually inclined. Madhyamaka points to the limitations of the intellect by rejecting and refuting all points of view. When all views are abandoned, one enters the experiential realm of shunyata.

The Madhyamaka School failed to provide a methodological framework for deepening its own penetrating intellectual insights. It was left to the Yogachara tradition in India, as the self-appointed corrective successor to Madhyamaka, to provide the methodologies to bring to fruition the insights of Madhyamaka. In China and Tibet, the most creative impulses of the Yogachara-Madhyamaka interaction gave rise to Zen and tantra, respectively, to provide meditational and doctrinal context for deepening the experience of shunyata, while remaining true to the paradoxical nature of the Madhyamaka insights.

Bodhidharma, the legendary Indian founder of Zen in China, is said to have given his robes, bowls, and a copy of the *Lankavatara Sutra* to Hui-ko, the second patriarch, as symbols of transmission of the lineage. Thus, it would seem that the *Lankavatara*, a Yogachara text, ought to be most closely associated with the later philosophical developments in Zen; instead we find that over centuries, the *Diamond* and the *Heart Sutras* have become the two most revered, influential, and commonly recited texts in Zen monasteries throughout east Asia.

Brevity may have been a decisive factor in the adoption of these texts by the Zen sect. In the case of the *Diamond Sutra*, the verse at the end:

So you should see [view] all of the fleeting world:
A star at dawn, a bubble in the stream,
A flash of lightning in a summer cloud,
A flickering lamp, a phantom, and a dream.

has been an inspiration for countless generations of Zen Buddhists. A similar place of honor is accorded the final verse of the *Heart Sutra: Gate gate paragate parasamgate bodhi svaha.* In both cases, while the influence of mantra religiosity is quite clear, it nonetheless highlights the Mahayana inclination to replace a thousand sermons with a single poem, an inclination still more pronounced in the Zen tradition where the distrust of language is so explicit.

The first noteworthy association we have of the *Diamond Sutra* with the Zen tradition is through the life of Hui-neng, the sixth patriarch, considered the real founder of the distinctly Chinese Zen tradition.[43] Whether legend or fact, the story of Hui-neng says that as a young boy he lived in extreme poverty and gathered wood to sell in the market to support himself and his mother. One day, in the marketplace, he heard a monk chant a phrase from the *Diamond Sutra* that said, "Let your mind function freely, without abiding anywhere or in anything." Upon hearing this phrase, the young boy was suddenly enlightened!

The *Diamond Sutra* figures again prominently in the Hui-neng legend when it is said that the fifth patriarch, Hung-jen (600–674) of the northern Zen school, expounded the sutra to Hui-neng and brought him to fuller awakening at the time of giving him transmission in the school and the robe of the patriarchate. The rest of Hui-neng's story is inseparable from the development of Zen in China and the history of Buddhism in east Asia. Among other things, Hui-neng's "awakening" experience, used by his student Shen-hui as a wedge in the rivalry between the "northern" and "southern" schools of Zen, began the controversy in the Zen tradition between sudden and gradual awakening, which has persisted to this day.

The second intersection of the Zen tradition with the *Diamond Sutra* is through the early career of Te-shan Hsuan-chien (782–865), one of the most celebrated Chinese Zen masters. Te-shan began his clerical career in Sichuan Province, in the southwest, and even as a young man attained mastery of the Prajnaparamita texts, especially the *Diamond Sutra*. He spent some twenty years reflecting upon and writing commentaries on the *Diamond Sutra.* Then he heard reports of a new cult in the far southeast where followers of the "sudden awakening teaching" sat facing a bare wall in order to see directly into their own buddha nature! Te-shan was full of righteous indignation—how could these people who neglect the study of the sutras aspire to buddhahood simply by seeing into their own nature?

Determined to put a stop to this heresy, he put all his commentaries on the *Diamond Sutra* in a backpack and set out on foot on a long journey to the far south. Arriving there, he stopped at a roadside tea shop and asked for some refreshments. These refreshments were, and still are, known as *mou mou*. As a play of words, the characters for *mou mou* can also mean "mind fresheners." The old lady who was the proprietor of the teashop playfully asked the monk what great treasure he was carrying in his backpack. Pridefully, Te-shan mentioned that he had spent twenty years writing these commentaries on the *Diamond Sutra* and that he was now on his way to teach the southern barbarians the true way to understand the Buddha's teaching. The old lady became reflective and said to Te-shan, "I have a question for you concerning the *Diamond Sutra*. If your answer can convince me, I will serve you the *mou mou* without any charge. But if you cannot, you may not be served."

Needless to say Te-shan was quite delighted to have this chance to prove his great scholarship. The old lady asked him, "In the *Diamond Sutra*, it says that one cannot get hold of the past mind, one cannot get hold of the future mind, and one cannot even get hold of the present mind. So, my question to you is which mind are you going to refresh?"

Te-shan was completely stunned. All his scholarship could not help him, and he was unable to answer the old lady. The chastened Te-shan did not eat his refreshments after all but asked for directions to the nearest Zen temple. This part of Te-shan's first encounter with Zen ends with him publicly burning his twenty years worth of scholarly writings on the *Diamond Sutra* in the temple courtyard the next morning. Te-shan went on to become one of the most celebrated masters in Zen history, and his life story remains one of the tradition's great anecdotes.

Te-shan's encounter with the old lady is one of the earliest examples of koan development in Zen. The hallmark of this development is a no-holds-barred approach, largely verbal but sometimes physical, which forces the listener to find meaning in his or her own inner experience, where an understanding of the situational context no longer depends on a textual or conceptual framework.

The Zen tradition has tried to comprehend this wisdom through the now formalized teaching of not-knowing. Not-knowing is the intuitive wisdom where one understands information to be just that—mere information—

and tries to penetrate to the heart of the mystery that language and information are trying to convey. All we have, in normal human conditioning, is second-, third-, or fourthhand information. In our ignorance, we treat these units of information as self-evident truths and fail to investigate our own experience directly. The not-knowing approach is not a philosophical or intellectual entertainment; it is a doorway to liberation.

The framework of not-knowing with which the Zen tradition works has *theopathy* but no theology (to restate the uneasy relationship between a spiritual experience and religious dogma). We find the same organizing principle at work in the *Diamond Sutra*. The paradoxical sayings of the *Diamond Sutra* presage the development of the koan method of practice in the Zen tradition. Developed in east Asia as a distinctly Chinese form of Buddhist meditation, the koan is an intentionally absurd formula whose purpose is to produce a liberating breakthrough in the mind of the meditator, that is, to shake the mind out of its linear, conceptualized ways of thinking. The puzzling, paradoxical sayings of the *Diamond Sutra* serve the same function and force listeners and readers to rearrange their conceptual framework.

Literary and Social Conventions
in the *Diamond Sutra*

J UST AS IN OTHER Buddhist sutras, the *Diamond Sutra* contains an abun-
dance of Indian literary conventions of respect embedded in the hier-
archical structure of Indian religiosity, such as how to address the Buddha
and how to requested his teaching. We also find numerous repetitive phrases, indicative of the remnants of the oral culture of ancient Buddhism. In
looking at the sutras as archeological treasures, we have to keep in mind
that even when they were written down, a Mahayana person, whether a
monastic or a lay practitioner, did not have access to more than one or two
sutras in his or her lifetime. Hence the practitioner's responsibility was to
memorize the sutra by heart and literally worship it as the body of the Buddha. The repetitive phrases undoubtedly helped this memorization process.

In keeping with the literary genres of its time, the linguistic formulations in the Mahayana sutras are rhetorical and exhortatory, baroque and
grandiloquent. No one has ever accused the Mahayana sutras of precision,
and the *Diamond Sutra* is no exception.

The style and the setting of the sutra are static, immobile, like a Noh
play. The tableau is set stiffly with no room for variation, but where a rich
exploration of nuances is possible. If we stretch our imagination, we may
even find a hint of *Waiting for Godot*, with Subhuti playing the straight man!

The *Diamond Sutra* generally follows the basic structure and linguistic
style of other Mahayana sutras:

> In fact, their [sutras'] style is a major defining characteristic of the
> [Mahayana] movement. Their surrealistic locales, measured in
> mind-boggling dimensions and filled with dazzling apparitions;
> their immense, all-star cast of characters; and the sheer extrav-
> agance of their language all serve to reassert the primacy of the
> visionary, shamanic side of Buddhism that had been generally

neglected by the Abhidharmists. Here, the seeming reality of everyday perception is viewed as a partial, limited way of experiencing a universe filled with multivalent levels so varied and complex that what seems real on one level dissolves into maya (illusion) on another. This has the effect of blurring the line between real and the illusory, making language seem totally inadequate for describing the truth. In this sense, the style of the expanded Sutras makes a graphic case for an assumption that underlies the Mahayana enterprise: Given the complexity of reality and the limitations of language, teaching can serve, at best, only as skillful means to effect a transformation in the mind of the listener/reader caught in the partiality of a particular view. Once the view has been discarded, the teachings designed to cure it should be discarded as well, to be replaced by other, perhaps seemingly contradictory, teachings appropriate for whatever new view the individual becomes attached to on the next level of practice. This view of language is so dominant in the Mahayana teachings that some texts even assert that the bodhisattva doctrine itself is simply a skillful means.[44]

A linguistic analysis of the *Diamond Sutra* shows a pattern of authoritative assertions that are immediately contradicted and, in fact, turn out not to be assertions at all, at least in the sense of the word as we understand it. This pattern of contradiction plays havoc with the conceptual order of language (a trait later appreciated with gusto by the Zen masters), reminding the reader that the text itself is merely an arrangement of words or verbal notations. It is linguistic deconstruction at its best—a caution against being seduced by rhetoric.

> The Sutra is a self-deconstructive text in so far as it underscores both its own status as a discursive phenomenon and the contradictions involved in mistaking its declarations for either literal or metaphorical truth....Thus in presenting language as an instrument of deception it seeks to unmask that deception and the motives which help to perpetuate it....If language functions to structure a homogenous 'self' and a 'world', then the Sutra functions to expose these two types of mental construct as contingent and arbitrary.[45]

A distinctive feature of Prajnaparamita-inspired wisdom is the awareness that language is inadequate to express the insights of an awakened consciousness that has managed a total extinction of the ego-self either through cognition (as in the case of Hui-neng) or through sustained meditational effort (as in the case of yogis.) The *Diamond Sutra's* use of language to destroy linguistic categories is intended to produce liberated cognition and finds parallel in modern deconstructionism.

> It is a post-structuralist commonplace that language constructs the reality it seems merely to refer to; therefore, all texts are fictions (some more useful than others), whether they acknowledge it or not.[46]

The current deconstruction theory undermines "logocentrism," or the belief that meaning inheres in the world independent of human attempts to represent it in words. It takes apart the logic of language in which authors make their claims and reveals how all texts undermine themselves because every text includes unconscious "traces" of positions exactly opposite to that which it sets out to uphold. The *Diamond Sutra* plays havoc with all attempts at creating meaning out of a certain order of words. For modern deconstruction, each person's universe is constructed by language, which then creates a particularized sense of reality that is, in fact, a cultural context; and the so-called reality is a "text" whose meaning is deciphered by infinite associations with other "texts." This finds parallel in the linguistic usage in the *Diamond Sutra* as well as the later Zen tradition, where the koan method seeks to deconstruct all "texts"—all preconceived notions of "reality"—so that the practitioner can stand as a naked witness to whatever is happening at that moment. But whereas modern deconstruction aims to free the mind from structures of meaning imposed from outside, simply for the sake of asserting one's right to one's own sense of context, Mahayana deconstruction aims to free the mind even from its own sense of context. Unlike the aimlessness of literary deconstruction, the aim of Mahayana deconstruction—whether in Nagarjuna or Zen—is to awaken the individual to the true nature of reality, not merely to play with words. The overriding concern of the *Diamond Sutra* is to use language and reasoning in paradoxical ways to free the listener from the "texts" of language and reasoning so that he or she may advance along a new, liberating way of seeing things.

In the *Diamond Sutra*, passages that seem like "grand narratives" or absolute claims are immediately discarded, paralleling postmodernity's skepticism toward such narratives. But here the discarding of seemingly absolute statements is in the service of producing a transformed "view" that is rooted in the practitioner's own direct experience. The play of words in the sutra is not for the sake of playing a game, but rather an attempt at perceptual revolution. This perceptual revolution is what the Buddha's teachings are all about.

PART II

The *Diamond Sutra:*
Translated Text and Commentary

THE TITLE Vajrachedika literally means "diamond cutter" or, in Buddhist usage, "sharp like a diamond, which cuts away all unnecessary conceptualization and brings one to the farther shore of awakening." Diamonds, once found extensively in India, are extremely hard gems. A diamond will not break into pieces, yet it will cut through all the other precious stones. In the days before machines, jewelers used diamonds to cut glass and other jewels. It is in the sense of prajna wisdom cutting through all delusions that the term diamond cutter is employed in the title of the sutra.

The image of cutting or cutting through is also reinforced by conventional iconographical depictions of the perfection of wisdom in which Manjushri, the celestial bodhisattva, holds the sword of wisdom with which he cuts through the spell of delusion. Equally significant is the depiction of two lotus blossoms at the level of his head, on each of which is placed a book of Prajnaparamita literature. In these iconographical representations, the lotus is symbolic of our true nature or buddha nature, which remains unstained by the defilements of the world (samsara), here represented by the root that grows from the mud. The lotus is also an identifying attribute of Avalokiteshvara, the bodhisattva of compassion. Thus the perfection of wisdom is identified iconographically with the sword of wisdom cutting through delusions and with the inherent compassion of the bodhisattvas. In a number of Madhyamaka texts, homage is paid at the beginning to Manjushri under the name of Manjughosa ("the gentle voiced") as the symbol of attaining enlightenment through intellectual insights. In Tibet, great scholar-monks like Tsongkhapa have been considered incarnations of Manjushri. In Zen iconographical representations, Manjushri and Avalokiteshvara, the symbols of wisdom and compassion, are seen as attendants to Shakyamuni Buddha.

As has been mentioned earlier, the date of composition of the sutra is generally considered to be about 350 C.E., in India. From the number of its verses, the sutra was also sometimes known as *Trishatika Prajnaparamita,* the *Perfection of Wisdom in Three Hundred Lines.* From the textual evidence, it seems reasonably certain that the teachings contained in this sutra are present in various guises in the larger Prajnaparamita texts of 100,000, 25,000, 18,000, and 8,000 lines. The chronological framework of the sutra supports the thesis that the teachings of the larger Prajnaparamita sutras were presented more succinctly through the *Diamond Sutra.*

SECTION I

Thus have I heard. At one time the Buddha was staying at Anathapindika's garden in Jeta Grove in the city of Shravasti. With him was a large gathering of 1,250 monks and bodhisattva-mahasattvas. Early in the morning, when the meal time came, the Buddha put on his robe and, holding his bowl, entered the great city of Shravasti where he begged for food. Having finished begging from door to door, he came back to his own seat in the garden and took his meal. When this was done, he put away his robe and bowl, washed his feet, spread his seat, and sat down, mindfully fixing his attention in front of him.

Thus have I heard: The Sanskrit original, *evam maya shrutam ekasmin samaye,* literally means "Thus did I hear. Once upon a time…" This literary convention is found appended to the beginning of each of the sutras in the Pali canon. According to tradition, immediately after the death of the Buddha, all the senior monks gathered together in the city of Rajagraha in the kingdom of Magadha to find common agreement on what the Buddha had taught during his lifetime. The site for the council was a cave on Vulture Peak near Rajagraha. This first council was presided over by Kasyapa, the most senior of the monks. It is important to keep in mind that not all monks traveled with the Buddha at all times; the Buddha had enjoined his monk-disciples to travel far and wide on their own in order to bring the Dharma to one and all. While they were on the road many of these monks received ongoing teachings of the Buddha through the grapevine and a network of satellite monk communities. It was, at best, filtered information. At the First Council, the elders decided to have a commonly agreed upon and fixed recension of Buddha's teaching. (As a historical footnote, it should be noted that no women or nuns were invited to attend the assembly.)

The monk Ananda was one of Buddha's chief disciples and his personal attendant during the last twenty-five years of his life. Although there is much uncertainty about his family history in various Buddhist textual traditions, he may have been the Buddha's first cousin. Ananda was also renowned for his prodigious eidetic memory. Kasyapa, the president of the Council, appointed Ananda as the main reciter of Buddha's words—hence the words "Thus have I Heard" at the beginning of each sutra in the Pali canon. Procedurally, Ananda would recite his version of what he had heard, and the other monks, if they were present at the time of that particular teaching of the Buddha, might offer amendments or additions; and thus would emerge the final version of each sutra, which would then be memorized and recited on a regular basis by the monks as part of the oral culture to which they belonged. Thus was formed the Sutrapitaka (the basket of Buddha's sermons) as one of the two baskets, the second being the Vinayapitaka (the basket of the rules of monastic conduct). The third basket, the Abhidharmapitaka, the compendium of Buddhist psychology, was not added to the canon until much later.

Because the material was so vast, there soon emerged a corpus of monks (*bhanikas* or reciters) who specialized in the memorization of different sections of the Sutrapitaka. In later years, very few monks, if any, memorized the whole Sutrapitaka.

In the case of the *Diamond Sutra*, the phrase "Thus have I heard" is clearly a literary fiction as the sutra was composed seven or eight hundred years after Ananda's lifetime. Adopting the same literary convention as the earlier Pali sutras was an obvious effort to legitimize the Mahayana sutras as the actual words of the Buddha. The Mahayana rationale has been that the phrase "Thus have I heard" is a generic phrase reflecting generational transmission in a teacher-to-student oral culture. The Mahayanist contention is that a number of teachings of the Buddha were kept secret because they were given only to advanced students and are to be found only in teacher-to-student transmission. Thus, for them, the phrase refers not to Ananda, but to the transcriber hearing the sutra from his (rarely her) teacher.

Shravasti: Shravasti, the "city of wonder" (now a ruined city in Uttar Pradesh in northern India), was a major metropolis in ancient India and the capital city of Koshala, which was one of the most powerful kingdoms of Buddha's time, ruled over by King Prasenjit for many years. The Buddha was apparently remotely related to Prasenjit, and the latter became one of the great patrons of Buddhism. Another great patron was King Bimbisara of the neighboring, and equally powerful, kingdom of Magadha (with its capital city at Rajagraha, in the present-day state of Bihar). The delicate balance of peaceful coexistence between these two powerful neighbors was upset when Ajatashatru, the son of Bimbisara and the new ruler of Magadha, invaded Koshala and added it to his empire, just prior to the Buddha's death.

Jeta Grove (Jetavana), just outside the city of Shravasti, is so called because the land originally belonged to Prince Jeta of the Koshala kingdom. It was bought for the use of the Buddha and his disciples by Anathapindika, a rich banker of Shravasti who was one of the earliest disciples of the Buddha and a great supporter of the sangha. When Anathapindika approached Prince Jeta for the purchase of the land, Jeta told the would-be buyer that he would sell the land only if Anathapindika covered it with gold coins, thinking that such a demand would deter Anathapindika. When Anathapindika actually started to cover the ground with gold coins, Jeta sought an audience with the king in order to have the transaction stopped, saying he didn't really want to sell the land. The king adjudicated, ruling that when Jeta named the price it was an offer to sell. Jeta relented and asked for one small area of land not to be covered by gold coins; he would offer that area to the sangha himself, he said. The remaining gold coins were then used to build the monastic dwellings.

The Buddha is said to have spent twenty rain retreats (during India's heavy monsoon months) of his teaching career at Jeta Grove. The canonical accounts show that Shravasti and Rajagraha were two major sites of Buddha's teaching activities.

A large gathering of 1,250 monks: Often a large group of monks traveled with the Buddha and stayed with him in ever shifting configurations and numbers. We have no firsthand evidence of these numbers, but the number 1,250 would seem to be a hyperbolic Indian literary convention to denote a substantial assemblage. It is not unlikely that at least several hundred gathered to hear the man who was probably the most famous religious teacher of his time in India.

Bodhisattva-mahasattvas: The Sanskrit version of the *Diamond Sutra* mentions the presence of bodhisattva-mahasattvas in the retinue along with the bhikshu sangha *(bhiksu-sataih sambahulais ca bodhisattvair mahasattvaih).* Thich Nhat Hanh, translating from the Chinese version, says explicitly that no bodhisattvas were present.[47] It seems to me that the Sanskrit text is more accurate and that the term bodhisattva is used here to refer generically to the followers of the Mahayana course, male and female, lay and monastic. Since the main thrust of the sutra is about the path of a bodhisattva, it becomes problematic to postulate that the sutra would have been preached without the presence of the bodhisattvas themselves. Thich Nhat Hanh's translation and interpretation seem to have a serious textual problem.

In Mahayana usage, the term bodhisattva automatically implies the conjunctive term bodhisattva-mahasattva to denote all beings who have taken the vow to be reborn—no matter how many times this may be necessary—in order to attain *samyaksambodhi,* the complete and perfect buddhahood for the benefit of all sentient beings. The word mahasattva literally means "great being." The implication in the use of the hyphenated term is that anyone who embarks on the bodhisattva path is a "great" or "superior" being. The Tibetans translate mahasattva as "great spiritual hero." At another level, the mention of mahasattvas would indicate that by the time of the writing of the *Diamond Sutra* the idea of the bodhisattva path was fully in place even if some of the doctrinal formulations were still being refined.

When the meal time came: This matter-of-fact statement is an eloquent testimony to the simplicity with which the Buddha lived his daily life. Even though he was a friend and spiritual adviser to kings and rich merchants, and for the most part surrounded by a large number of admiring disciples and followers, he insisted on going out himself every morning to beg for his food. Sometimes alone, sometimes accompanied by other monks, he would enter a village or town and go from house to house on the begging round. At times, onlookers couldn't tell the Buddha apart from the other monks—he walked barefoot, he wore robes made out of rags, and ate the same kind of alms food as his fellow monks.

Spread his seat, and sat down, mindfully fixing his attention in front of him: The daily routine of the Buddha, as it has come down to us through the Pali sutras, consisted of getting up very early in the morning, washing himself, and sitting in meditation until it was time to go on the alms round. After he had come back and finished his meal, he gave a Dharma talk to the assembly of monks and lay people from the village who might have brought food for him and the monks. It was the Buddha's custom to make himself available each morning after his meal and in the evening for answering questions that a monk or a visitor might have. His afternoon and evening sermons were attended by monks, nuns, lay followers, interested—and sometimes hostile—followers of rival religious sects, and the merely curious.

During the talks or sermons, the Buddha would formally sit in a meditation posture and fix his attention on the breath. It was in this state of equipoise, of balanced concentration and wisdom, that the Buddha listened to the questions asked of him and expounded on them. In this state of awareness the Buddha transcended the merely intellectual and logical states of mind and accessed the infinite mode of consciousness-being. The answers given by the Buddha are an expression of prajna—highest intuitive wisdom. The effort of the Mahayana sutras, especially the *Diamond Sutra*, is to emphasize this infinite mode of consciousness-being.

In the early afternoon, the Buddha rested briefly and then took a bath. After coming back from the bathhouse he would be available to any monk or nun who wished to consult him. Some asked questions on meditation subjects, and some requested to hear the Dharma. This would go on until the early part of the evening. Legends tell us that in the middle watch of the night (10 P.M.–2 A.M.) the gods of the entire ten thousand world-systems had the opportunity to consult the Buddha. In the last watch of the night (2 A.M.–6 A.M.), the Buddha lay down and rested mindfully.

It was a well-regulated and simple life in which the Buddha created a balance between solitude and interaction with the community of monks and visitors. It was a life of pure conduct and utmost simplicity, devoid of pretensions. Although brought up in the manner of an aristocrat, he spoke the local dialect and interacted with everyone in complete sincerity. It was a mind completely purified, totally at peace, free of any form of sorrow, lamentation, pain, grief, and despair, devoid of greed, craving, attachment, ill will, or aversion. This purity of life and conduct made the Buddha the role model in the quest for awakening.

The simplicity of Buddha's daily life has fundamental implications for followers of his teachings. In the earliest strata of the Pali sutras there is a strong current of rejection of metaphysical speculations. What is emphasized is the peace and joy that come from abstaining from conflicts—religious, social, political. Conflicts are bred by clinging to views and opinions; in the Buddha's system, the ultimate renunciation is letting go of all views.

A great man would not grasp onto and dispute those [views],
free from which he should conduct himself in the world.[48]

SECTION 2

Then the Venerable Subhuti, who was among the assembly, rose from his seat, bared his right shoulder, set his right knee on the ground, and, respectfully folding his hands, addressed the Buddha thus: "It is wonderful, World-Honored One, that the Tathagata thinks so much of all the bodhisattvas and instructs them so well. World-Honored One, in the case of a son or daughter of a good family, who arouses the thought for the supreme awakening, how should they abide in it and how should they keep their thoughts under control?"

The Buddha replied, "Well said, indeed, O Subhuti! As you say, the Tathagata thinks very much of all the bodhisattvas and instructs them well. But now listen attentively and I will tell you how those who have set out on the bodhisattva path should abide in it, and how they should keep their thoughts under control."

"So be it, World-Honored One. I wish to listen to you."

The manner of this request by Subhuti is highly stylized and is common to all the Mahayana sutras; it may even have been common to all sects of any religious persuasion during the time of the Buddha. Certainly there are enough mannerisms in contemporary Hindu religious culture to indicate that these formal ways of interacting with a teacher may have belonged to the larger religious culture of India of the Buddha's time.

Subhuti: A disciple of the Buddha who is said to have excelled in the meditation of loving-kindness. He is also said to have been the "foremost among those dwelling in peace" (Pali: *arana-viharinam aggo*). The word *arana* is used here to denote "dwelling in peace." Conze says of the word *arana* that it is has multiple meanings:

> …[the word] may denote freedom from strife, battle, or fighting i.e. harmlessness; or it may also mean that Subhuti lived in solitude, retired from the world, in a remote forest, in quietude and peace. A man is "peaceful" if he has inward peace of mind and if he behaves peacefully toward others. Subhuti's deep insight is the fine flower of his friendly behavior.[49]

Subhuti gets little mention in the Pali tradition; he is mentioned as being the younger brother of Anathapindika, the donor of Jeta Grove to the sangha of the Buddha. It is said that on the day of the dedication of Jeta Grove, he heard the teaching of the Buddha and was ordained as a monk. He lived in the forest for long periods of time and developed insights based on the practice of loving-kindness. In the Prajnaparamita sutras Subhuti is a major bodhisattva figure and is shown as deeply knowledgeable in the teaching of emptiness. There may be an intentional symbiotic relationship here in that the setting of the sutra has an intimate connection with Subhuti's family history. In the Avadana literature, Subhuti is also presented as practicing (and advocating) *buddhanussati* (recollection of the qualities of the Buddha) above all other meditation themes. As this was one of the primary meditation themes in early Mahayana, this may explain Subhuti's prominence in Mahayana literature.

Bared his right shoulder, set his right knee on the ground...: Both of these customs are most likely pre-Buddhist Indian religious rituals. The custom of monks saluting the feet of the Buddha with their head is reflected even today in Buddhist monks bowing three times in front of a Buddha image or in front of their teacher or a senior monk. The custom of circumambulating the Buddha, keeping him to one's right, is also preserved to this day. The custom of a monk baring his right shoulder was also adopted when formally addressing the Buddha to ask a question, as a mark of respect. It showed that one did not have a weapon concealed in one's hand. This practice may have been common to all religious sects of the time. There were similar customs and etiquette at the royal courts.

A historian of Buddhist sainthood calls these patterns of behavior "a veritable grammar of devotion."

> Thus there is a somewhat informal pattern of general (cultic) behaviors that people are to employ in the presence of the living Buddha: one is to rise, greet him respectfully, offer him a seat, circumambulate him and prostrate oneself to him, present water for his feet as well as food and drink, make other offerings such as flowers, hold a parasol over him to shield him from the elements, ask after his health, make confession, praise him, express one's commitment as a devotee, request teachings, listen respectfully, follow his instructions, and so on.[50]

World-Honored One: One of the polite forms of address for respected spiritual teachers in ancient India. Here it literally means a teacher who is respected and honored throughout the known world.

Tathagata: Literally, "one who has become real" *(tatha agata)* or "truly gone" *(tatha gata).* It has been variously translated as "thus gone," "thus come," "thus perfected." The Buddha realized the true nature of things, their "suchness" or *tathata*. Therefore he became one of the rare beings who is called a Tathagata. It is an epithet used in ancient India for a person who has attained the highest religious goal. In Buddhism, it usually refers specifically to the Buddha although occasionally it also refers to any of his disciples who have attained the level of arhat. It is also used as one of the ten titles of the Buddha, which he himself used when speaking of himself or other Buddhas.

Tathagata is a term of much scholarly debate within the Buddhist tradition. In the Yogachara formulation of the three bodies *(trikaya)*[51] of the Buddha, Tathagata refers specifically to the Buddha in his nirmanakaya aspect. He is the perfected being who can take on any form and who possesses the ten powers of a Buddha and also the cosmic principle, the essence of the universe, the unconditioned. He is the intermediary between the essential and the phenomenal worlds. In the absolute sense, the word Tathagata is often equated with prajna and shunyata. In such a sense, a Tathagata does not suffer from entropy, the inexorable running down of an energy system.

Here, in the *Diamond Sutra*, the term Tathagata is used in the sense that the skill with which the Tathagata imparts his teachings in the human world helps remove the impediments that may have threatened the spiritual development of a bodhisattva in an earlier time.

A son or daughter of a good family: This expression, a translation of the Sanskrit term *kulaputra*, is a polite form of address, but its usage may also refer sociologically to the class consciousness of the Buddha's sangha. As noted earlier, a majority of the Buddha's disciples came from the new and prosperous class of merchants and professionals. Its use here may suggest a lingering desire for respectability among the shramanas (whom the Buddha and his earliest disciples considered themselves to be) in their complicated relationship with the entrenched Brahmin priesthood. Tradition tells us that a number of young men and women from Brahmin families became disciples of the Buddha and joined his order. In the centuries after the passing away of the Buddha when there was a struggle among the Buddhists, the Jains, and the Ajivikas for patronage from kings and merchants, it might have been crucial to have among their ranks "sons and daughters of good family" rather than just a motley collection of recruits from the lower classes.

Supreme awakening: This is the attainment of full buddhahood or the awakening of a perfect Buddha. This realization is called *anuttara samyaksambodhi* and is characterized by the overcoming of all defects and the possession of omniscience and the rest of the ten powers *(dashabala)* of a perfected Buddha. In Mahayana this is the goal of the bodhisattva path. We will encounter this term again and again throughout the sutra.

SECTION 3

The Buddha said to Subhuti, "All the bodhisattva-mahasattvas, who undertake the practice of meditation, should cherish one thought only: 'When I attain perfect wisdom, I will liberate all sentient beings in every realm of the universe, whether they be egg-born, womb-born, moisture-born, or miraculously born; those with form, those without form, those with perception, those without perception, and those with neither perception nor non-perception. So long as any form of being is conceived, I must allow it to pass into the eternal peace of nirvana, into that realm of nirvana that leaves nothing behind, and to attain final awakening.'

"And yet although immeasurable, innumerable, and unlimited beings have been liberated, truly no being has been liberated. Why? Because no bodhisattva who is a true bodhisattva entertains such concepts as a self, a person, a being, or a living soul. Thus there are no sentient beings to be liberated and no self to attain perfect wisdom."

All sentient beings in every realm of the universe: The Buddhist cosmological conception introduces us to a vast universe, challenging our ingrained notion of a human-referenced, self-limiting universe. Buddhist tradition accepts three realms in which a consciousness may exist: human, subhuman, and divine. In this formulation, one form of life is no more or less important than the other, although the human realm, with its unique possibility of reformulating basic intentions, is clearly the most propitious in terms of striving for liberation from samsara.

Buddhist teachings envisage four kinds of birth by which beings are born into the six modes of existence. Birds and reptiles are egg-born; mammals and humans are womb-born; worms, insects, and butterflies are moisture-born (generated from humidity); the miraculously born are those who appear all at once, without conception or embryonic growth. This last category includes the *deva* (gods), *preta* (hungry ghosts and other infernal beings), *naraka* (hell beings), and beings in the intermediary worlds.

The schema of six modes of existence *(gati)* identifies three "good," or higher, and three "bad," or lower, modes of existence. The good modes are those of gods (further subdivided into twenty-six realms), titans, and humans. The bad modes of existence are animals, hungry ghosts and other infernal beings, and hell beings, said to belong to eight great hells of increasing intensity of torment. In traditional Buddhist cosmology there are thus thirty-one realms of existence.

The only difference among the various modes of existence is the degree to which the karmic process is being purified (in the sense of residual defilements being uprooted). Life is not without limit in any of these modes. Each human being has been animal, ghost, hell being, and god in the past, and is likely to be so again in the future if the karmic process is not totally extinguished. The human realm is considered the most fortunate because it is only in this realm that there is an awareness of the urgency to work on one's karmic residue and strive for awakening. While the Buddhist tradition speaks of the "precious human body" and the "precious human birth," it does not treat the universe anthropocentrically, that is, human existence is not seen as the sole reference point.

The gods live in the fortunate realms of the heavens but are, like beings in other realms, subject to rebirth. They have a very long and happy lifespan as a result of their previous good deeds. This may seem glamorous, but it is, in fact, a hindrance because in their unblemished happiness they cannot recognize the truth of suffering or strive for full awakening. Also, it is important to note that the tradition does not use human time as a frame of reference.

Those with form, those without form: Various realms of existence based on different states of consciousness have been pretty well mapped out in Abhidharma, the traditional compendium of Buddhist psychology. In this interpretation, the external universe

> is an outer reflection of the internal cosmos of the mind, registering in concrete manifest form the subtle gradations in states of consciousness. This does not mean that the Abhidharma reduces the outer world to a dimension of mind in the manner of philosophical idealism. The outer world is quite real and possesses objective existence. However, the outer world is always a world apprehended by consciousness, and the type of consciousness determines the nature of the world that appears. Consciousness and the world are mutually dependent and inextricably connected to such an extent that the hierarchical structure of the realms of existence exactly reproduces and corresponds to the hierarchical structure of consciousness.

Because of this correspondence, each of the two—the objective hierarchy of existence and the inner gradation of consciousness—provides the key to understanding the other. The reason why a living being is reborn into a particular realm is because he (or she) has generated, in a previous life, the kamma or volitional force of consciousness that leads to rebirth in that realm, and thus in the final analysis all the realms of existence are formed, fashioned, and sustained by the mental activity of living beings. At the same time these realms provide the stage for consciousness to continue its evolution in a new personality and under a fresh set of circumstances.[52]

Those with perception, those without perception: Beings with perception are those with sense organs, while beings without perception are a class of devas who live in the higher realms of existence (specifically, realms number twenty-one to twenty-seven). There are even higher realms (numbers twenty-eight to thirty-one) of the so-called immaterial sphere plane. The highest of these realms—the apex of Buddhist cosmology—is the realm of "neither perception nor non-perception."

Nirvana that leaves nothing behind: Buddhist tradition distinguishes between two kinds of nirvana—with substratum and without substratum. The term nirvana stands for "nirvana *with* substratum" and denotes the awakening experience in which all defilements have been irrevocably uprooted. Still, the five skandhas remain and continue to experience the arising and passing of thoughts, feelings, sensations, and so forth, but these experiences leave no imprint on the consciousness. Hence no defilements ever take root.

The term *parinirvana* stands for "nirvana *without* substratum" and means that the consciousness is no longer subject to rebirth in this or any other world. This is different from mere bodily death. The bodily death of an unenlightened being continues to propel the habit formations through an endless round of rebirth and death due to residual imprints on the consciousness. The bodily death of an enlightened being, on the other hand, means entering into nirvana without substratum (here understood as final cessation), thus freeing the consciousness forever from the rounds of rebirth and death. This was the earliest interpretation of the parinirvana of Shakyamuni Buddha. What happens to the consciousness thus freed remains a much-debated and much-speculated area of Buddhist scholarship and meditational traditions.

One of the earliest notions in the development of Mahayana, first articulated in the Lokottara School, a subschool of Mahasanghika, was that Shakyamuni Buddha, upon his physical death, did not enter parnirvana in the sense understood by other early Buddhist schools, but rather entered into *mahasamadhi* (literally, great concentration, eternal presence) and continues to exist as dharmakaya. This notion of nirvana without substratum became a key element in the changing status of the Buddha in early Mahayana. In later developments, it is in his dharmakaya aspect that Shakyamuni Buddha continues to guide all bodhisattvas on the path of anuttara samyaksambodhi (the perfect unexcelled enlightenment) so that they may, in turn, continue to guide sentient beings along the path of nirvana.

Although immeasurable…truly no being has been liberated: With these words the heart of Prajnaparamita is laid bare through the core teaching of shunyata. The genius of Mahayana was to postulate the mutual identity and interdependence of samsara (the world of conditioning) and nirvana (the unconditioned) in that both are characterized by shunyata. The famous line from the *Heart Sutra* encapsulates this paradox: "Form does not differ from emptiness, emptiness does not differ from form. That which is form is emptiness, that which is emptiness is form."

Earlier we discussed the term shunyata. What follows here is a brief discussion of the mutual identity of samsara and nirvana (in Mahayana, nirvana is often equated with shunyata, hence the overlapping of the two terms.) When looked at from the perspective of shunyata doctrine, nirvana has no independent existence of its own. This understanding is admittedly at odds with the Abhidharma understanding whereby nirvana exists in its own right as an unconditioned dharma.

In the Prajnaparamita sutras, nirvana is synonymous with shunyata and stands for the subjectless, objectless knowing of the nature of reality, which is neither an entity nor a separate region and which is without any substantial foundation.

Lex Hixon has translated the term prajnaparamita to shed light on the meaning of shunyata:

> The unthinkably deep realization of the bodhisattva is to abide without abode, to dwell where no objective or subjective structures can dwell—without any underlying physical or metaphysical foundation. This spontaneous and foundationless dwelling in isolation from every abstract world view is of infinitely greater value than any religious teaching or contemplative experience.[53]

The creative paradox inherent in the teaching of shunyata is at the core of the Mahayana tradition. It simultaneously holds the vision of two levels of truth—the relative and the absolute—and sees the two informing each other. The *Heart Sutra* and the *Diamond Sutra* are the most eloquent expressions of this paradox. The Zen tradition inherited this mantle and re-expressed the core of these teachings in a distinctive way. Hixon describes the interplay of the relative and the absolute in this way:

> The relative truth of existence is that it is an expanse of suffering beings, a condition which is the motivation for the precious Mahayana commitment to universal conscious awakening. This relative truth of suffering must not be swallowed up, even subtly, by the absolute truth that Reality is an inherently selfless expanse, an infinite, empty space, intrinsically peaceful and blissful. Relative truth and absolute truth must remain in subtle balance or even in perfect unison.[54]

He goes on to express most eloquently the responsibility we must assume for ourselves in this interplay of the relative and the absolute:

> Philosophically, this paradox means that we must uphold, protect and even exalt the coherent functioning of relative structures, beings and events, no matter how insubstantial they are from the standpoint of absolute truth. Our own reincarnational careers as continuous mind streams and the moral imperative of universal compassion upon which these careers eventually come to be founded are not some form of illusory existence. In fact, because it is the proper sphere of compassionate action, the relative becomes more prominent, more spiritually charged, than the absolute.[55]

If form is emptiness, if samsara and nirvana have a mutual, interdependent identity, how does one find a balance living in the world? Mahayana Buddhism emphasized the notion of skillful means as the middle way between wisdom (of the essential emptiness of all forms) and compassion (for the suffering in the realms of forms). The bodhisattva, in his or her infinite wisdom, sees the emptiness of all phenomena yet also sees that human beings are caught in greed, hatred, and delusion, and thus remain forever in the bondage of samsara unless help is provided. The bodhisattva has compassion for their plight but also perceives that, in an absolute sense, there is no one who is in bondage. The bodhisattva treads the path of skillful means, forever finding appropriate responses through wisdom and compassion. Although the bodhisattva works tirelessly to emancipate all beings, in his or her wisdom of emptiness, he or she knows that ultimately no beings truly exist and hence no beings are ever emancipated.

A self, a person, a being, or a living soul: In the *Diamond Sutra* the use of the four terms self *(atman)*, person *(pudgala)*, being *(sattva)*, and living soul *(jiva)* is a rhetorical device whose aim is to disabuse the reader of any notion of an abiding entity to be found anywhere. The self is the supposed center around which our sense of ownership is organized: "this is mine; I am this; this is me." A person is what is observed from the outside as a social entity—it is the self-identification that results from the role one plays in each environment. Buddhist teachings see the term "person" as no more than a conventional name for a conglomeration of physical and psychological elements that change from moment to moment and have the appearance of unity. A being is the sense through which an individual separates what seems to be inside from what is outside the self—the separation of subject and object, the experiencer and the experienced. A living soul is the unifying source of an individual's life, the embodied self that identifies with the body and the mind.

In effect, all four terms are synonyms for a sought-after essence that is imperishable and that makes its appearance in different incarnations where it retains some semblance of continuity. The Buddha's teaching of no-self or anatman was a revolutionary stance within the context of the religious beliefs of his time. He questioned the existence of an independent, imperishable, unchanging essence anywhere in the mind-body system of the individual, but he did not go so far as to assert that there is no psychic continuity. Contrary to popular belief, he did not teach a nihilistic doctrine of "no-soul," which would have rendered the issues of ethics and wholesome conduct completely irrelevant. What he proposed was a personal investigation of the two extreme beliefs of "soul" and "no-soul" and seeing both of these beliefs as mere points of view that lead to attachment and suffering. His teaching of the "middle way" is to see all deterministic points of view as erroneous.

The *Diamond Sutra* rejects the trajectory of human conditioning that moves from (1) unexamined assumptions (atman) to (2) linguistic usage of unexamined assumptions (pudgala) to (3) firmly held beliefs (sattva) based on linguistic usage of unexamined assumptions to (4) identification (jiva) with such beliefs. The wisdom of the bodhisattva is to perceive that all four terms are mere linguistic usage and that nothing corresponding to them is to be found anywhere.

In shunyata there can be no idea of a dharma or a no-dharma, both being linguistic constructs. In the same way, a person, an ego-self, a soul, and a being are linguistic constructs. In actual experience, mind-states are arising and passing away with great rapidity without any permanent entity experiencing those mind-states. For a bodhisattva to be caught in these concepts would mean to be caught in delusion.

SECTION 4

"Furthermore, Subhuti, in the practice of generosity a bodhisattva should be unsupported. He or she should practice generosity without regard to sight, sound, touch, flavor, smell, or any thought that arises in it. Subhuti, thus should a bodhisattva practice generosity without being supported by any notion of a sign. Why? When a bodhisattva practices generosity without being supported by any notion of a sign, his or her merit will be beyond conception. Subhuti, what do you think? Can you measure the space extending eastward?"

"No, World-Honored One, I cannot."

"Subhuti, can you measure the space extending toward the south, or west, or north, or above, or below?"

"No, World-Honored One, I cannot."

"Subhuti, so it is with the merit of a bodhisattva who practices generosity without cherishing any notion of a sign; it is beyond measure like space. Subhuti, a bodhisattva should persevere one-pointedly in this instruction."

In this section the *Diamond Sutra* refers to the six perfections of the bodhisattva: generosity *(dana)*, ethical conduct *(shila)*, patience *(kshanti)*, effort *(virya)*, meditation *(samadhi)*, and wisdom *(prajna)*. A number of texts in the Prajnaparamita group expound on each of these perfections in detail. The *Diamond Sutra* uses the perfection of generosity to encapsulate all the other perfections. Conze, after Vasubandhu's commentary, says that

> the perfection of giving includes all others. The giving of *material things* then represents the perfection of giving in its narrower sense; the giving of *protection* results from the perfections of morality and patience; and the gift of the *Dharma* corresponds to the perfections of vigor, meditation and wisdom.[56]

Although the *Diamond Sutra* and other Prajnaparamita sutras expound the perfections as traversing the path of bodhisattvahood, it talks about them through the prism of the overarching perfection of shunyata—as a process-oriented movement rather than a goal. Although the term "perfection" is used in the *Diamond Sutra*, its meaning is quite different from the linguistic usage. It is a perfection that does not aim at completion; rather, it is wisdom based on practice through which one is always progressing toward the ideal.

The emphasis on generosity also comes from earlier Avadana literature where acts of generosity are represented as prime factors in spiritual progress. Also, calculation of merit is a recurrent theme in Avadana literature. In this and in other ways we see how the *Diamond Sutra* is trying to work out the themes already present in Avadana literature.

Should be unsupported: The scope of the Sanskrit term *apratishtita* mirrors the core message of the *Diamond Sutra*. Conze has translated it in a number of ways as follows.

    A. As applied to relations between two objects or forms or bodies:
        1. Not relying on anything
        2. Unsupported by anything or unsupported anywhere
        3. Not depending on anything or nothing to be depended upon
        4. Not standing about anywhere
        5. Not established anywhere
        6. Not carried [away] by anything
        7. Not fixed on anything
        8. Not resting on anything
        9. Not leaning on anything
      10. Not holding on to anything
      11. Not abiding in anything or not intent on anything abiding anywhere
      12. Not attached to anything
      13. Not clinging to anything
    B. As applied to emotional experience:
      14. Not settling down anywhere
      15. Not making oneself at home anywhere
      16. Not seeking a secure base anywhere
      17. Not seeking any refuge or security anywhere
      18. Not rejoicing in anything
    C. As applied to social relationships:
      19. Not expecting any help from anything

20. Not trusting in anything (except perfect wisdom)

21. Not believing [blindly] in anything[57]

It is hard to imagine a more uncompromising declaration of nonattachment and renunciation. As we shall see, this non-attachment is the central thrust of the sutra.

Without being supported by any notion of a sign....: "Sign" or "mark" (Pali: *nimitta*) is a technical term for the object of false perception. At times it is identified as a defilement. Of necessity, nimitta belongs to the realm of forms, not of shunyata. A person who entertains the notion of nimitta is someone who misperceives the nature of reality and imagines that indicators point to actually existing things. The opposite of such misperception is true perception in which phenomena are seen to be empty and not existing in their own right. Linguistically, the opposite of nimitta is *animitta*—"signless" or absence of characteristics in all dharmas. It stands for the absolute, which is devoid of all distinctions.

When generosity is practiced through this true perception, there is no investment in the outcome of the giving. The bodhisattva here is enjoined to forget about him- or herself and about the rewards that may accrue as a result of meritorious deeds. This is the mind of giving everything over to others without any thought of giver or receiver. The practice of the perfection of giving thus offers a new way to transform and transcend the basic notion of duality—myself versus others—that leads to separation of oneself from others and continues the notion of a separate self. The fruit of this training is to live one's life without barriers or limitations. The linguistic paradox in the sutra is, of course, the declaration that the merit of generosity is incalculable.

It is beyond measure like space: The bodhisattva's selfless, altruistic practice of generosity (and the other perfections) is compared to space because it is all-pervading, vast, and without measure. However, it must not be assumed that the practice of generosity is an absolutist goal, or that it can override the prajnaparamita, the wisdom of shunyata. What it means, in effect, is that the practice of each of the perfections should be undertaken as an open-ended, process-oriented engagement, making each of the perfections a "mean," a tool for an altruistic and undeluded life, enabling one eventually to complete the bodhisattva path and attain buddhahood.

SECTION 5

"Subhuti, what do you think? Is it possible to recognize the Tathagata by means of bodily marks?"

"No, World-Honored One. And why? When the Tathagata speaks of the bodily marks, he speaks of the no-possession of no marks."

The Buddha said to Subhuti, "All that has a form is an illusory existence. When the illusory nature of form is perceived, the Tathagata is recognized."

This section continues the discussion on the "possession" of signs or marks (by a form). In Mahayana Buddhism, as in earlier Buddhism, the final stage of attaining buddhahood is equated with the acquisition of the thirty-two bodily marks and the ten powers of the anuttara samyaksambodhi. Just as it is a mistake to look for "signs" in things, so it would be a mistake to look for the thirty-two bodily "signs" of the Buddha in order to recognize him.

Traditionally, the cultivation of the path of the bodhisattva means that after a long period of striving through many lifetimes, the bodhisattva comes into "possession" of all the thirty-two bodily marks that indicate his or her buddhahood. The idea here is that these bodily marks are a result of countless altruistic meritorious deeds, but at the same time it would be a delusion to believe that the six perfections should be practiced simply in order to attain them.

If all forms are empty at their core, what, in an ultimate sense, would "possess" the thirty-two marks? The teaching of the sutra here is that even the form of the Tathagata is empty, transitory, illusory, not worth clinging to. The Tathagata, as dharmakaya, is a frame of reference, not a bodily form, which by nature is illusory; they have no reality of their own, being informed as they are by causal interdependence. To recognize all forms as inherently empty is to recognize the Tathagata as a frame of reference rather than as a bodily form.

The doctrine of trikaya, literally, of "the three bodies of Buddha," is predominantly associated with the texts of the Yogachara school, the third great school of Indian Mahayana Buddhism (after Prajnaparamita and the Madhyamaka schools). The Yogachara texts became instrumental in the rise of esoteric branches of Buddhism, both in India and elsewhere. A number of schools in Tibet, for example, derive their lineage primarily from Yogachara (the Nyingma sect in particular), as do the schools of Shingon, Kegon, and Tendai in Japan.

The idea of trikaya is, however, present in embryonic forms in Prajna-paramita literature. The three bodies of the Buddha are the dharmakaya or "dharma body," the sambhogakaya or "bliss body," and the nirmana-kaya or "phantom body." Both the sambhogakaya and the nirmanakaya are projections of the dharmakaya.

The nirmanakaya is the body of the historical Shakyamuni Buddha, visible to ordinary human beings and intended to inspire people to embark on the path of Dharma. The nirmanakaya is the proactive aspect or projection of the dharmakaya in the phenomenal world; it is an act of reimagination of a Buddha in the ordinary world. The nirmanakaya operates in human time.

The sambhogakaya is the subtle, quasi-material body, neither a fully relative nor a fully absolute body through which the Buddha guides highly developed practitioners on the path of buddhahood. Sambhogakaya is also translated as "communal enjoyment body," which communicates the idea of sharing in the joy of a community both in causal and effective modalities. It operates in non-human time. In later Mahayana/Yogachara developments, the notion of sambhogakaya served as an ideal whereby practitioners could engage in visionary experiences that are essentially shamanic at their core. In cosmological formulations, the sambhogakaya came to be associated with a number of celestial Buddhas and bodhi-sattvas. In Vajrayana, the depiction of the sambhogakaya became a complex iconographical phenomenon. In this perspective, the sambhogakaya is seen as an archetype, a symbolic representation of certain qualities of buddhahood.

The dharmakaya is the unformed, unmediated, primordial consciousness. It is a synonym for ultimate reality itself, the final development of buddhahood, an abstract resolution of all dualities (in shunyata), beyond any conceptualization or designation. The dharmakaya is beyond time and space.

The basic notion of the trikaya doctrine is that Buddhas operate simultaneously in the conventional and absolute realms. It might be more accurate to say that their consciousness remains grounded in a realization of shunyata and the ultimate nondual nature of reality even as they engage in the world of appearances and conventional reality. Thus they do not get caught in karmic formations for themselves.

There is a discussion of the thirty-two marks of the Buddha in the *Lakkhana Sutta* of the Digha Nikaya in the Pali canon. A belief in these thirty-two marks combined with several outside factors may have contributed greatly to the rise of devotionalism in Mahayana. The first of these factors is that around the time of the beginning of the common era, in northwestern India, under Greek and Mediterranean influences, Buddha statues were sculpted for the first time. In early Buddhism, as in the contemporaneous Upanishad literature, we find that the idea of a personality cult was frowned upon. In ancient India the veneration of a holy person took the form of worshipping a memorial shrine *(stupa)* rather than a physical image. The second factor is that the renaissance in Hinduism at the grass-roots level, at about the same time that the *Diamond Sutra* was composed, introduced ever more vigorous devotional elements into Indian society from which various Buddhist schools could not afford to isolate themselves.

It may also have been the case that devotionalism was a pan-Indian phenomenon, and both the Buddhists and the Hindus had a role in developing it. An influence of Nestorian Christianity on this trend cannot be ruled out. There may have been a persistent concern among the early Mahayanists about the thirty-two marks—after all, this was one of the crucial differences between the Buddhas and the arhats. As architects of an alternate to the arhat model, the early Mahayanists may have focused on texts like the *Lakkhana Sutta* to give them guidelines on how to follow the path to buddhahood. The intention of the authors of the *Diamond Sutra* may have been to take a more elitist stance, which is in keeping with the consistent effort of the sutra to guard the doctrine of the absolute against misunderstandings.

Yogachara also introduced the notion of alayavijnana, "the storehouse consciousness," to address the issues of continuity in consciousness. Another term synonymous to alayavijnana, tathagatagarbha, literally, "the womb of the Tathagata," is now firmly embedded in the Yogachara. Scholars speculate, however, that this term may have originated outside the Yogachara, but, once inside, it got conflated with dharmakaya and alayavijnana. In any case, both of these terms are of critical importance in later Mahayana/Yogachara developments and are outside the scope of this commentary. But in a nutshell, tathagatagarbha/dharmakaya might be called the ground of being, or a place from where all things emerge. In this sense, this notion is very similar to the enfolded order in quantum physics. Alayavijnana is the place where each imprint on consciousness or "seed" gets mixed up with countless other imprints in unimaginable ways, and re-emerges into the unfolded order in a completely new reconfiguration.

Section 6

Subhuti said to the Buddha, "World-Honored One, in times to come, will there be beings who, when they hear these teachings, have real faith and confidence in them?"

The Buddha: "Subhuti, do not utter such words. Five hundred years after the passing of the Tathagata, there will be beings who, having practiced rules of morality and being thus possessed of merit, happen to hear of these statements and will understand their truth. Such beings, you should know, have planted their root of merit not only under one, two, three, four, or five Buddhas, but under countless Buddhas. When such beings, upon hearing these statements, arouse even one moment of pure and clear confidence, the Tathagata will see them and recognize their immeasurable amount of merit. Why? Because all these beings are free from the idea of a self, a person, a being, or a living soul; they are free from the idea of a dharma as well as a no-dharma. Why? Because if they cherish the idea of a dharma, they are still attached to a self, a person, a being, or a living soul. If they cherish the idea of a no-dharma, they are attached to a self, a person, a being, or a living soul. Therefore, do not cherish the idea of a dharma nor that of a no-dharma. For this reason, the Tathagata always preaches thus: 'O you bhikshus, know that my teaching is to be likened unto a raft. Even a dharma is cast aside, much more a no-dharma.'"

Five hundred years after the passing of the Tathagata…: This polemical exchange has to be seen in the light of the historical debate between the earliest Mahayana followers and Nikaya Buddhism. The Mahayanist claim was that the Abhidharma corpus had turned the Buddha's teachings into something dry and stagnant and that their own movement was an attempt at a regeneration of those teachings. The Vinayapitaka section of the Pali canon contains a saying attributed to the Buddha that the true dharma will last only for five hundred years after his death.[58] This statement has been interpreted by Nikaya followers to mean that the "true Dharma" would be adulterated by an "improved Dharma" five hundred years after the passing away of the Buddha. The question of an adulterated Dharma versus regeneration of the Dharma was understandably a touchy issue between Nikaya Buddhists and the early Mahayanists. Also, whether or not the prediction was meant to forecast the appearance of Mahayana teachings remains unclear. But it was in the second century c.e., five hundred years after the death of the Buddha, that Nagarjuna, the philosopher-monk considered by the Mahayanists to be the second Buddha, lived and founded the school of Madhyamaka philosophy.

The emergence of the Madhyamaka School gave the erstwhile follow-ers of the Prajnaparamita texts the philosophical tools to engage in ongoing internal debates with their Abhidharma rivals, particularly the Sarvasti-vadins. From the Mahayana perspective, however, Madhyamaka was much more than that. It was a creative reinterpretation of Buddha's insights that allowed his Dharma to refashion and regenerate itself.

Have planted their root of merit…: We can read into Subhuti's question and the Buddha's response a statement of doubt and a reassurance respec-tively. Every generation of Mahayana believers has had doubts about the appearance of a future Buddha in corrupt times, or what the Hindus call the *kaliyuga* or dark ages. The Buddha's response to Subhuti, that there will be beings who have planted their roots of merit under countless Bud-dhas, is also an Avadana idea. The Avadana "pattern" requires that for an aspiration to arhatship or buddhahood to succeed, one must plant seeds of merit in buddha fields, and that the act must be recognized by the Bud-dha in question. The Buddha will then prophesy success at some future time. Note that this pattern follows the prophecy made by Buddha Dipankara in the case of Shakyamuni Buddha himself when he was the novice monk Sumedha.

In Mahayana sutras, it is a tenet that each Mahayana follower is a bodhi-sattva who has planted the seeds of merit through good deeds over many lifetimes. More specifically, he or she has at some point had the thought of helping others; some have aroused bodhichitta, the thought of becom-ing a Buddha in order to help others. The past deeds of a bodhisattva include ethical conduct; venerating the Buddhas of the past; doing mer-itorious deeds in the presence of the Buddhas; cutting off false notions with regard to persons and dharmas; developing deep, abiding faith; train-ing extensively in ethical conduct, concentration, wisdom, and so on.

According to Mahayana, when such beings arouse even one moment of pure faith in the teaching of the sutra in the present, it validates and re-establishes the fruit of all the practices they have done in the past. When these beings listen to the teaching of the sutra without getting caught in the idea of an ego-self, a person, a living being, or a soul, their immea-surable merit (continued from the past) rediscovers its locus through trust in the Tathagata.

This clearly is a soteriological device and emphasizes the importance of faith and trust. On one level it is asking the bodhisattva to have faith in the teaching of the Buddha, but, on another level, it is asking for trust in one's own buddha nature. In Mahayana, the Buddha and his teachings are not outside one's own innate buddha nature—they are all part of the fabric of tathagatagarbha or dharmakaya.

If they cherish the idea of a dharma...[as well as] a no-dharma...: Following Madhyamaka dialectic, shunyata is the middle ground between affirmation and negation, between "is" and "is not." A true bodhisattva does not cling to the notion of either dharma or no-dharma. Outside of its practical application as upaya, any discussion of dharma or no-dharma falls into the category of conceptual or metaphysical speculation. Such speculation is not the concern of a Buddha or a true bodhisattva.

Thus the celebrated Zen master Huango-po Hsi-yun (d. 850 c.e.) could throw our conceptual thinking into a vortex by declaring,

> The fundamental dharma of the dharma is that there are no dharmas, yet that this dharma of no-dharma is in itself a dharma; and now that no-dharma dharma has been transmitted, how can the dharma of the dharma be a dharma?[59]

My teaching is to be likened unto a raft....: In the earlier discussion on skillful means we saw how the metaphor of the raft has been used as a potent image in the Buddhist tradition, dating from the early texts. These lines in the sutra reassert that all of Buddha's teaching is like a raft—skillful means—not a description of reality, not an ideology. Any grasping of the teachings as an ideology can only become another foolish possession. To try to cling to dharma or no-dharma is a foolish endeavor.

SECTION 7

"Subhuti, what do you think? Has the Tathagata attained the supreme awakening? Has he something he can preach?"

Subhuti said, "World-Honored One, as I understand the teaching of the Buddha, the Buddha has no doctrine to convey. The truth is ungraspable and inexpressible. It neither is nor is not. How is it so? Because all noble teachers are exalted by the unconditioned."

Has the Tathagata attained the supreme awakening?: Only a Tathagata can know the nature of supreme awakening, as all ordinary human knowledge is dualistic. The supreme awakening of the Tathagata consists precisely of transcending this duality. Also, only a Tathagata knows when this duality has been transcended or "attained." Even then the Tathagata knows the essential nature of both the transcendence and "attainment" to be empty. Hence, in a real sense, there is no attainment.

The prajnaparamita, being wisdom beyond words, is a truth that can only be intuited, not intellectually grasped. A Buddha does not teach a doctrine as an a priori belief system, hence the Buddha has no doctrine to preach. The caution here is to not set up Dharma as an object of knowledge that can then be conveyed to others. The human mind is easily infatuated with what it thinks it knows and tries to establish that knowledge as a statement of truth.

While prophets in most religions declare that they have the truth and that only their truth must be preached, the Buddha rejects any such notion. Here we come again to the notion of the teaching as a raft only, to be discarded as soon as one reaches the other shore. Each person must discover the truth for him- or herself and as soon as there is a realization it must be abandoned as a thing in itself lest one turns it into an ideology for oneself.

The Buddha had a direct realization of the truth in the hour of his awakening, but there was no way he could communicate his own experience to others. What he taught during the forty-five years of his teaching mission was a universal diagnosis of the human condition as characterized by dukkha (unsatisfactoriness) and a prescription for transcending this condition. Repeatedly he cautioned that what he taught must not be taken on faith, but that its veracity must be tested by each person through his or her own experience. The *Kalama Sutra* from the Pali canon is an eloquent testimony to the Buddha's insistence on this verification of the truth through individual, direct experience.

> Now, look you Kalamas, do not be led by reports, or tradition, or hearsay. Be not led by the authority of religious texts, nor by mere logic or inference, nor by considering appearances, nor by the delight in speculative opinions, nor by seeming possibilities, nor by the idea: 'this is our teacher'. But, O Kalamas, when you know for yourselves that certain things are unwholesome (akusala), and wrong, and bad, then give them up and when you know for yourselves that certain things are wholesome (kusala) and good, then accept them and follow them.[60]

Sangharakshita, a contemporary scholar of Buddhist history, rightly points out that we tend to take Buddhist teachings as abstract metaphysical ideas, "as if the Buddha propounded them for our intellectual consideration."[61] The evidence of the Pali sutras suggests that all of Buddha's efforts are directed toward a direct experience, not ideas mediated by our intellectual consideration.

Because all noble teachers are exalted...: The nobles teachers are exalted or ennobled by their experience of the unconditioned. Here the unconditioned is equated with emptiness. All noble teachers have tasted this emptiness, but as it cannot be put into words, the words they teach are used as skillful means, pointing to the possibility of reaching the unconditioned beyond dharmas and no-dharmas.

SECTION 8

"Subhuti, what do you think? If a son or daughter of a good family should fill the three thousand chiliocosms with the seven precious treasures and give them all as a gift to the Tathagatas, would not the merit thus obtained be great?"

Subhuti said, "Very great, indeed, World-Honored One. Why? Because their merit is characterized with the quality of not being merit. Therefore, the Tathagata speaks of the merit as being great."

The Buddha: "If there is a person who, memorizing even four lines from this sutra, preaches it to others, his merit will be superior to the one just mentioned. Why? Because, Subhuti, all the Buddhas and their supreme awakening issue from this sutra. Subhuti, what is known as the teaching of the Buddha is not the teaching of the Buddha."

Three thousand chiliocosms: A "chiliocosm" is a kind of galactic system that, according to Vasubandhu, consists of one billion worlds (Buddhaghosa, however, states that it consists of a trillion world systems).[62] Three thousand multiplied by a billion gives us a mind-boggling number. It is even more impossible to try to conceive of the many universes in space. However, a recent news item in the *New York Times* reporting the discovery of the largest galaxy ever detected puts these cosmological numbers in some perspective. The discovery was made by astronomers using the thirty-six-inch telescope at Kitt Peak National Observatory in Arizona.

Including more than 100 trillion stars and measuring more than six million light years in diameter, the galaxy is 60 times the size of Earth's own galaxy, the Milky Way…. The newfound galaxy is located in the center of an even larger clump, a cluster of some 1,000 galaxies called Abell 2029… Since there doesn't appear to be enough ordinary matter in the universe to account for the huge gravitational forces that would seem necessary to cause all the clumping, scientists propose the existence of vast amounts of invisible matter that eludes detection because it emits no radiation. According to the prevailing wisdom, some 99 percent of the universe consists of this missing mass, which means that what is generally thought of as astronomy actually concerns only a tiny subset of particles that happen to be detectable by the human nervous system.[63]

Mahayana practitioners claim that the cosmological numbers in the *Diamond Sutra* are not a mere metaphor but come from a cosmic eye that clearly sees how the universe is constructed. At the very least, the use of these incomprehensible numbers is meant to transcend the limitations of boundaries created by ordinary thinking. These lines function in the *Diamond Sutra* as a heuristic device to bring home the idea that in a true act of generosity there is no intention of one's giving or the other's receiving and no separation between the giver and the receiver. In the act of ordinary giving there is some calculation as to the value of the gift, and the quality of the recipient. Irrespective of what the gift may be, there is always some element, however subtle, of self-interest.

The seven precious treasures: In normal calculation, the seven most precious gifts are gold, silver, coral, gems, diamonds, pearls, and lapis lazuli. The most exalted of all recipients is the Tathagata. According to a deluded perspective, the gift of these precious jewels to the Tathagata will thus accrue the most merit. But with prajna one can clearly see the evanescence of these gifts as compared to the true gift that comes from teaching even four lines from the *Diamond Sutra* whereby one's listeners too may be helped along the path of nirvana. In these lines we see a subtle shift from the Avadana literature, which is typically concerned with the calculation of merit to be obtained through gifts to the Tathagata, to the Prajnaparamita literature, which emphasizes the gift of Dharma/prajna above all.

Would not the merit thus obtained be great?: Merit, in the traditional Buddhist sense, is the benefit or mechanism that ensures a happier and more comfortable life in the future. The idea of gaining merit was firmly entrenched in pre-Buddhist India in Vedic culture where hereditary priests presided over ritual sacrifices for the benefit of military and political patrons. The self-reliance of the shramana culture was a challenge and an affront to the power of Brahmin priests and provided a backdrop of rival claims for merit-making and eventual "awakening" in each teacher's "Dharma."

The idea of merit-making has played a central role in Buddhist history and the question of why lay people would want to support monastics through the donation of material goods is really no different in Buddhism than in any other religion. Never an imperial religion in India, Buddhism devised a variety of ways to cultivate the symbiotic relationship between the donors of material goods and the dispensers of spirituality. The Pali canon makes it clear that the gift of Dharma surpasses all other gifts. The issue of merit-making comes up again and again in the *Diamond Sutra*, and one cannot help thinking that there must have been a creative tension in the Buddhist culture of the time between the need for merit-making on a material level (even monks have to eat) and the implications of shunyata—between the giver and the receiver. We must remain cognizant of this creative tension when we consider the teaching in Mahayana (as well as in the larger Buddhist tradition) that the practice of six perfections has numerous benefits, both in this life and the next.

It was not long after the time of the Buddha that Buddhist monks became an alternative focal point for the accumulation and transference of merit. The books of *Vimanavatthu* and *Petavatthu* in the Khuddhaka Nikaya sections of the Pali texts contain numerous stories highlighting this development.

> That the lay-people lived in close proximity with monks was of great advantage to them. For monks, regarded as great fields for merit, *punna*, in the world, gave laity ample scope and opportunity to make merit by receiving the gifts they gave with reverence and a mind of faith. The kammic effect, even if it fell short of attaining nibbana, the state that moves and changes not, was yet a rebirth in a sphere where, in marked contrast to the poverty, the difficulties, struggles, obligations and duties of life on earth, was one where there was light, rest, pleasure and beauty, and absence of responsibility. Here, in "Mansions", merit done, helped it may have been by the compassion and understanding perhaps of the Buddha himself, perhaps of his monastic followers, is shown to result in a lifespan spent in a

glorious, mobile Mansion in a deva-world. Thus is demonstrated as a main theme at least one aspect of kamma-vipaka, deed and fruition.[64]

In the Mahayana Pure Land school that found great success in China, merit-making was linked directly to aspiration for rebirth in Amitabha's western paradise, which was an extension of a trend already present in Indian Nikaya Buddhism—formless consciousness in a god realm. Alternatively, merit-making may have provided greater opportunities for spiritual advancement. Merit is generally spoken of as a "heap of merit" in the belief that it accumulates over many lives and has a cumulative effect. This popular belief is highlighted in the Avadana literature where the cumulative effect of meritorious deeds is emphasized over and over again.

The issue of merit is linked to the career or path of the bodhisattva who, through countless meritorious deeds over numerous lifetimes, acquires the thirty-two marks of the supreme Buddha. In reality, however, this heap of merit is "no heap" because all its constituents are empty—just as all other compounded entities or heaps are empty. This paradox—whereby it is declared that there is no merit even while practitioners on the bodhisattva path are exhorted to acquire it—exemplifies the tension at the very heart of Mahayana tradition.

This paradox in the *Diamond Sutra* foreshadows the famous interview between Emperor Wu of South China and Bodhidharma, the legendary founder of the Zen tradition. According to Bodhidharma's legend, when the patriarch first appeared at the emperor's court, the monarch told him how many temples he had had built, how many monks and nuns he had supported, and how many sutras he had copied, some with his own hands. "What," he then asked the bearded monk, "do you think is the merit of all this great work?" "None whatsoever, your majesty," replied Bodhidharma, without missing a beat!

The Buddha says in the *Diamond Sutra* that whatever merit may be acquired from the gifts of precious jewels and other objects to exalted persons, if someone were to teach and explain even one four-line stanza of this sutra to someone else, the merit from that act would be much greater than any imaginable material gift.

Memorizing even four lines…: In a fashion typical of the Mahayana sutra literature, the evangelical fervor of the Mahayana followers shows through here. The merit accrued from teaching a *gatha* or stanza of four lines from this sutra is much greater than the gift of all the precious jewels in the world, so they declare. The enterprise of the Prajnaparamita sutras is to insist on the insight of shunyata—its realization and its teaching to others.

It is not immediately clear whether any four-line stanza or a particular stanza is meant in this paragraph, but it is in keeping with another initiative of the Prajnaparamita tradition: the promotion of the cult of sutras. We see in this devotional development a revolt against certain elitist trends that were present in Indian religiosity long before the *Diamond Sutra* was composed and recall the revolt of the shramanas against the Brahmin priesthood whose entrenched power was based on mnemonic training. A parallel elite developed within Buddhist schools where reciters (Pali: *bhanikas*) specialized in memorizing specific portions of the sutras (hence the division of the Nikaya section into five different parts.) The aspiration of the average spiritual seeker in any religion has always been at odds with the specialization of the religious elite. Here the *Diamond Sutra* clearly states that memorizing even one stanza from the sutra with a heart full of devotion and conviction is of greater merit than that of the professional memorizer.

We have already seen how Hui-neng, the sixth patriarch of Zen, came to an awakening as a young boy on hearing a monk chant a stanza from the *Diamond Sutra*. We find a number of similar stories in Zen history, and it seems to follow from these incidents that really any stanza from this sutra has equal power to bring forth an awakening. Or, we can look at the last stanza of the sutra as its definitive encapsulation in which the sutra points, in poignant and dramatic terms, to the nature of samsara: fleeting, transient, and ephemeral and marked by suffering, impermanence, and soullessness. Awakening means abandoning clinging to this impermanent world; everything in the realm of the relative must be understood as such.

All the Buddhas and their supreme awakening: Continuing the evangelical fervor, this section insists that listening to this sutra with complete sincerity can spark awakening. From the perspective of the absolute it would be a mistake to call this sutra a teaching of the Buddha because the wisdom of shunyata transcends all Buddhas; it is timeless, it is the basic law or Dharma of the universe, regardless of whether Buddhas appear in the world or not. Perhaps on one level it is a criticism of the earlier texts, such as the Abhidharma with its tendency to categorize. On another level this sentence may be saying that all Buddhas teach the wisdom of shunyata and, as such, this teaching is not specific to any one Buddha. The Buddhas teach shunyata not to create yet another category, but to point to a timeless truth.

Section 9

"Subhuti, what do you think? Does a srotapanna think, 'I have obtained the fruit of srotapatti'?"

Subhuti said, "No, World-Honored One, he does not. Why? Because while srotapanna means 'entering the stream,' there is no entering here. A true sro-tapanna is one who does not enter sound, odor, flavor, touch, or any thought that arises."

"Subhuti, what do you think? Does a sakridagamin think, 'I have obtained the fruit of a sakridagamin'?"

Subhuti said, "No, World-Honored One, he does not. Why? Because while sakridagamin means 'going and coming just once,' one who understands that there is really no going-and-coming, he or she is a true sakridagamin."

"Subhuti, what do you think? Does an anagamin think, 'I have obtained the fruit of an anagamin'?"

Subhuti said, "No, World-Honored One, he does not. Why? Because while anagamin means 'not coming,' there is really no not-coming; therefore the one who realizes this is called an anagamin."

"Subhuti, what do you think? Does an arhat think, 'I have obtained arhat-ship'?"

Subhuti said, "No, World-Honored One, he does not. Why? Because there is no dharma to be called arhat. If, World-Honored One, an arhat thinks, 'I have obtained arhatship,' this means that he has the idea of an ego-self, a person, a living being, or a soul.

"Although the Buddha has said that I am the foremost of those who have obtained aranasamadhi, that I am the foremost of those arhats who are lib-erated from unwholesome desires, World-Honored One, I cherish no thought that I have attained arhatship. World-Honored One, [if I did] you would not have declared of me, 'Subhuti, who is the foremost of those who dwell in peace-ful abiding, does not dwell anywhere; that is why he is called a "dweller in peace.""

Srotapanna/sakridagamin/anagamin/arhat: This is the fourfold classi-fication in Nikaya Buddhism of awakening to the transcendent path and its fruits. These four terms are translated as "stream-winner" "once-return-er," "non-returner," and "worthy one," respectively. The stream-entry schema refers to the stages of progress on the path and the fruit of the holy life at each stage. It was a crucial ingredient in the formation of the early Buddhist world-view.

In Nikaya Buddhism a *srotapanna* or stream-winner is one who has transcended the first three fetters (belief in self-identity, skeptical doubt, and attachment to mere rules and rituals). He or she enters the stream of nirvana and is no longer subject to rebirth in the lower, subhuman realms. Such a person is firmly established on the path to awakening and will pass through no more than seven rounds of rebirth in the heavenly and human realms before attaining final awakening, thus putting an end to suffering forever.

A *sakridigamin*, a once-returner, is someone who has in addition weakened the fourth and the fifth fetters of sensual passion and irritability. Such a person will be reborn only one time either in the heavenly or the human realm before attaining final awakening.

An *anagamin* or non-returner has become fully free from the abovementioned five lower fetters. After death such a person reappears in the highest Brahma worlds and reaches nirvana without ever returning to this world.

An *arhat* or saint is one who has become free from the five still subtler fetters: passion for form, passion for formlessness, conceit, restlessness, and ignorance. An arhat is said to attain final emancipation in this very life.

The *Diamond Sutra* makes a consistent effort to deconstruct assumptions in the stream-entry schema through the prism of shunyata and to insist that the four categories do not exist in reality. True stream-winners are those who understand the illusory nature of the categories.

Historically, this passage may also be seen as Mahayana engagement in an ongoing debate with the Pudgalavadins or the Personalitists, an important school of Nikaya Buddhism whose members were quite numerous and influential at the time of the composition of the *Diamond Sutra*. The Pudgalavadins advanced the notion of a "person" who exists outside the five skandhas or "heaps" of form, feeling, perception, impulse, and consciousness, but claimed that this person is neither identical with nor different from the five skandhas.

I cherish no thought that I have attained arhatship....: Referring to himself, Subhuti says that although the Buddha has declared him to be the foremost among those arhats who have attained *aranasamadhi* (dwelling in utmost peace), he is free from the illusion that he has attained anything. This follows the pattern in the Pali canon where arhats indicate their realization by not referring to an "I." Subhuti seems to be saying here that he does not concretize the thought of attaining arhatship and is therefore not liable to the danger of trying to grasp it.

SECTION 10

The Buddha asked Subhuti, "What do you think? When the Tathagata practiced in ancient times under Dipankara Buddha, did he attain any Dharma?"

"No, World-Honored One, he did not attain any Dharma while practicing with the Dipankara Buddha."

"Subhuti, what do you think? Does a bodhisattva create any harmonious buddha fields?"

"No, World-Honored One, he does not. Why? Because to create a harmonious buddha field is not to create a harmonious buddha field, and therefore it is known as creating a harmonious buddha field."

"So, Subhuti, all bodhisattvas should develop a pure, lucid mind that doesn't depend upon sight, sound, touch, flavor, smell, or any thought that arises in it. A bodhisattva should develop a mind that functions freely, without depending on anything or any place."

The line of argument continues here from the previous section, this time through a reference to one of the Buddha's own previous lives. The story of Shakyamuni Buddha's novitiate under Dipankara, the first of the twenty-four Buddhas preceding the historical Buddha, is an important story in the *Nidanakatha*, "The Story of the Lineage." Dipankara Buddha is said to have lived an immeasurably long time ago. It was in the presence of Dipankara that the future Shakyamuni Buddha, at that time a young monk named Sumedha, made the great vow to become a Buddha. Through his supernatural powers Dipankara recognized that after an immense number of ages had passed, Sumedha would become a Buddha named Gautama.

Create any harmonious buddha fields: As mentioned earlier, arousing bodhichitta, or the "thought of awakening," is synonymous with the vow to attain full buddhahood for the benefit of all beings. To do so in the presence of a Buddha is the first step on the path of the bodhisattva. It is an initiatory rite, so to speak, in sowing the buddha fields.

The realms in which the Buddhas reside and teach are not an entirely new Mahayana idea for we find the term "buddha field" *(buddhakshetra)* in pre-Mahayana texts. The Avadana literature uses the term in the sense that each Buddha functions as a "field" in which seeds of merit, when sown, yield extraordinary good results. The notion of seeing all the buddha fields, however, does appear to be a Mahayana innovation. The term is also translated as "buddha land." This term refers to a place where a celestial Buddha resides. It became one of the Mahayana's most potent ideas.

While the spiritual journey of the bodhisattva is the completion of a psychological and emotional matrix—the emergence of a fully integrated human being, within the Mahayana tradition that is only half the story. The other half is a parallel dimension of reality in which is recognized the existence of many invisible worlds and entities not yet acknowledged by science.

As we have seen, Buddhist texts from all strata provide four models of the perfected human being: arhats, pratyekabuddhas, bodhisattvas, and samyaksambuddhas. Although the Nikaya tradition sees Shakyamuni Buddha as a wise teacher and a diagnostician, a number of trends present even during his lifetime suggest the future creation of a larger-than-life personality. Various accounts in the Pali sutras attest to Buddha's ability to access events beyond time and space. Within the context of Indian religious modality, this automatically accorded him more than mere mortal status. In the India of Buddha's time, anyone who could see into the past and future was accorded saintly status and deemed worthy of respect and veneration. It was then simply a matter of transferring the then current patterns of worship—ritual offerings, recollection of the names, and pilgrimage—to such a person.

In the earliest Buddhist communities, the recollection of the names or epithets of the Buddha probably represented the first stage of transforming the Buddha from a mere historical figure into one of mythic dimensions. It is said that Upali, one of the ten great disciples of the Buddha, uttered one hundred epithets praising the Buddha immediately upon becoming an ordained follower.

> Upali spoke these epithets spontaneously, as an expression of his faith and respect. Over the centuries the enumerations of these and other epithets focused on the extraordinary aspects of the Buddha's person, on his marvelous nature. In so doing they became a foundation for Buddhist devotional literature, their enunciation a support of devotional and contemplative practice.[65]

These epithets are the beginning of the hagiographic, mythic tradition in Buddhism of which the creation of celestial Buddhas and bodhisattvas is but a natural extension. Although this transition may sit uneasily with Western Buddhists, one needs to keep in mind that by the time of the emergence of the Mahayana in India, the devotional movement around the cult of Vishnu was also gaining strength among the Hindus. The emergence of the cult of Amitabha Buddha as a parallel devotional movement in Indian Mahayana may have been a response to these Hindu models while also an elaboration of tendencies already embedded in the tradition itself.

As a movement that found its inspiration in devotionalism rather than in the analytical minutiae of Abhidharma, Mahayana was not content merely with creating the bodhisattva archetype as distinct from the arhat and the pratyekabuddha ideals; it also distinguished between earthly bodhisattvas and celestial or transcendent bodhisattvas. The creation of cosmic deities in Hindu Purana literature took place at about the same time as this development in Mahayana.

The earthly bodhisattvas embody altruistic compassion as well as the cultivation of bodhichitta. The transcendent bodhisattvas, however, have actualized the perfections over many eons and have attained buddhahood but have postponed their entry into complete nirvana. They are in possession of perfect wisdom and are no longer subject to rebirth. But they continue to exist in extrahuman realms and assume many skillful means in order to help sentient beings on the path to awakening.

The noble and beneficent bodhisattvas in the pantheon of Mahayana cosmology are objects of veneration and devotion. The best known of these transcendent bodhisattvas are Avalokiteshvara (also called Padmapani), the bodhisattva of compassion; Manjushri, the bodhisattva of wisdom; Vajrapani, destroyer of negative formations; Kshitigarbha, the guardian of purgatories who is seen not as a torturer but as the superintendent of a model prison, doing his best to make life tolerable for his charges; he is also a protector of deceased children; Mahasthamaprapta, who brings to human beings the knowledge necessary for attainment of awakening; and Samantabhadra, protector of all those who teach the Dharma and the embodiment of the unity of nirvana and samsara.

The premise that there could be other Buddhas in other world systems was always embedded in Buddhist cosmological perspectives. The notion of the Buddhas of the past and future as well as extrahuman realms of consciousness is fully present in the Pali canon. The idea of Buddhas existing in other world systems was first articulated in the *Lotus Sutra*, making it perhaps the most influential sutra in east Asian Mahayana Buddhism.

Mahayana developed early notions of the supernatural and the sacred that guaranteed an exalted status to the symbols of its mystical and ethical ideals. Its notion of extraordinary beings populating supernal buddha fields and coming to the aid of suffering sentient beings necessitated a metaphysic and cosmology that could offer concrete images of a transcendent sacred. Accordingly, the abstract apophatic concept of emptiness was often qualified by, or even rejected in favor of, positive statements and concrete images.[66]

As we have already seen, the idea of multiple world systems is already present in the Pali canon's "thousandfold world system."[67] The Mahayana filled those worlds with iconographical representations of transcendent and sacred beings in a development that was to have enormous implications for the future of the tradition in east Asia and Tibet.

Though Mahayana and Nikaya Buddhism agree that the world is full of sorrow and suffering, the Mahayana is more optimistic. The presence of transcendent bodhisattvas represents hope for those believers who, for whatever reasons, cannot work on their own for awakening and wish to seek the help of fully liberated, compassionate beings.

In the *Ratnakuta Sutra*, perhaps the earliest document recording the training of the bodhisattva, the journey of all celestial Buddhas and bodhisattvas is said to begin with the arousing of bodhichitta. In Mahayana, bodhichitta is used both in the sense of a determination to become a Buddha as well as the actual state of awareness of a Buddha. Bodhichitta is one of the key concepts in later Mahayana and is often equated with buddhahood as well as tathagatagarbha. Implicit in this understanding is the notion that each "bit" of bodhichitta contains, in a way, all of buddhahood, as in a hologram.

The Zen tradition encapsulates this holographic aspiration in poetic and graphic terms. The four great vows are part of daily recitation in all Zen monasteries. The first of these vows says: "All beings, one body, I vow to liberate." From the Mahayana perspective this vow works on several levels. A deeper understanding of it reveals the core teachings of the tradition because it shows the nonseparation of individual beings from one another; all beings are viewed as a single body that is not different from one's own body-being. The aspiration to liberate one's body-being is intimately linked to the awakening of all body-beings because one contains the many, and the many comprise the one.

This holographic model finds striking parallels in quantum physics where an electron is found to be not one thing but a totality or ensemble enfolded throughout the whole of space much like shunyata or dharma-kaya in Mahayana. A Bohmian interpretation of the phrase "all beings, one body" would be to see this process of interaction as a "holomove-ment," which tries to convey the dynamic and ever active nature of incal-culable "enfoldings" and "unfoldings" that create our universe moment by moment.

The interface between Buddhism and science is an exciting new occur-rence in our time. Both religion and science have the tools, if used prop-erly, to approach the vastness and mystery of the universe in ways that affirm our sense of interconnectedness. In her ground-breaking book that compares the teaching of mutual causality in Buddhism and General Sys-tems Theory in science, Joanna Macy explores the systems view of reali-ty, arising in our century from biology and extending into the social and cognitive sciences. She finds:

> As the pattern-building interactions of phenomena were stud-ied, a different kind of causality came into view, one that is mutual, involving interdependence and reciprocity between causes and effects. Such a notion, which is an anomaly within the linear paradigm that has dominated Western culture, bears striking similarity to the Buddhist teaching of causality...[68]

Furthermore

> ...reality itself, in the systems view is dynamic, flowing, ever breaking upon us like the waves of the living sea. And the cog-nitive system, the mind, rides it by the continual process of per-ceiving and elaborating meanings.[69]

The systems view of reality—that it is dynamic, mutually caused, and interdependent—finds resonance in the Buddhist understanding of real-ity, which has always seen the microcosm and the macrocosm as reflecting each other. Everything in the universe is interwoven, and the bodhisattva archetype is an expression of that. This way of thinking has enormous potential for the future of the earth as a single, integrated ecosystem. Dam-aging one part of the planet means endangering the whole planet. This planetary awareness, both ecological and holographic, finds its parallel in the wisdom teaching of Indra's Net in the Hua-yen School (based on the *Avatamsaka Sutra*) of the Mahayana tradition.

> Because a dust-mote is [identical with, or is] an
> expression of the ultimate Reality, it can therefore
> contain all things.... Since all the universes con-
> tained within a dust-mote are also expressions of
> Reality, they too contain all other universes...this
> observation goes on indefinitely, and thus realms-
> embracing- realms *ad infinitum* are established. An
> illustration of this truth can be seen by either the
> demonstration of the interreflection of mirrors, or by
> the metaphor of the marbles of Indra's Net...[70]

Quantum physics holds that at the quantum level there is nothing other than energy and information. Each particle binds an incredible amount of energy, as witnessed, for example, on the cosmic level in the spectacle of streaking comets, burning stars, and scattering radiation. At the same time, each particle, though its composition is extremely complicated, carries information about the fundamental laws that govern its behavior at the elementary levels. The quantum field is the field of pure potentiality and it is influenced by attention, as seen in experiments where the mere act of observation alters the behavior of the particle in unpredictable ways.

On a material level, human beings share the same basic elements such as oxygen, hydrogen, and nitrogen with, for example, a tree and are thus part of the same quantum field. At the level of attention and its attendant intention, however, human beings have a much greater potential for man-ifesting the unmanifest. Because human consciousness is infinitely flexible, it is capable of expanding the boundaries of its awareness endlessly to include and influence all areas of energy and information in the quantum field.

If we transpose the quantum physics model to Buddha's awakening experience, we can say that the field of awareness of the the fully awak-ened Buddha or Tathagata became infinite and was able to access all infor-mation about past and present beings, the specifics of their repeated rebirths, and the patterns of interdependent origination each being shares with all others in the universe. To put it another way, the consciousness of the Tathagata covers the entire quantum (cosmic) field and is capable of influencing any or all parts of it through intention and attention. A celestial bodhisattva is an embodiment of the same field of awareness and establishes the intention to guide all beings caught up in samsara.

Physicists allow that in the quantum field there are no boundaries, no hard edges. Energy and information flow into each other without impediments. Each quantum reference point is instantly connected with all other quantum points holographically. The ebb and flow of energy and information in the quantum field is porous and uncontained. Although beings, visible and invisible, may be a manifestation of this quantum field, the field itself is not limited by their manifestation. In the Yogachara formulation, the dharmakaya similarly is not limited by the manifestation or lack of manifestation of beings in the field. In that sense, the Yogachara view finds resonance in the quantum field equation; energy and information (in the storehouse consciousness) are transformed through attention and intention (of the bodhisattva).

Moving from this contemporary understanding of the field of consciousness of a celestial bodhisattva to its development in the Pure Land tradition, we find that a number of practices were suggested to ensure rebirth into one of the numerous buddha fields or lands. Sukhavati and Abhirati are the two best-known buddha fields.

In the *Sukhavativyuha Sutra*, one of the core texts of the Pure Land tradition, we find the forty-eight vows of the bodhisattva Dharmakara before he became Buddha Amitabha. The Sukhavati buddha land was created as a result of these vows, and into it will be reborn all those who pray to Amitabha for relief. The sutra also includes a description of the features of this pure land; practices required of the aspirants for rebirth; the nature of existence in Sukhavati; and the attainment of buddhahood.

Earlier we referred to the rise of devotionalism in India in the second or first century C.E., when a number of devotional practices were incorporated into Mahayana, and new sutras were written to justify them. There is reason to believe that visualizing Buddhas and buddha fields was a particularly potent religious practice for Buddhists during the formative period of Mahayana in India. Just as Shakyamuni Buddha chose to live in our world for the benefit of all beings, there have been other Buddhas with similar attainments who continue to exist on a celestial plane where they provide visionary experience and inspiration to inhabitants of those realms.

Mahayana elaborated upon the notion of Buddhas of the past, present, and future consistent with the notion of "human time." These Buddhas are, respectively, Dipankara Buddha, Shakyamuni Buddha, and Maitreya Buddha. Although the Pure Land practices became oversimplified in China over a period of centuries, the earlier Indian conceptualization through the Mahayana sutras provided a framework for buddha fields and the vows of the bodhisattva. These vows, seemingly much more difficult to maintain and develop than the eightfold path of Nikaya Buddhism, were what moved followers to call Mahayana the "maha" or "great" vehi-cle. Explicit in these vows is the development of virtuous thoughts and a rigorous ethical conduct as a first step in one's perfection of the vows that will eventually lead to rebirth in one of the pure lands. This rebirth becomes the basis for perfecting anuttara samyaksambodhi, or perfect buddhahood.

The trajectory thus moves from 1) the arousing of bodhichitta to 2) the perfection of bodhisattva vows over many lifetimes to 3) rebirth in a pure land to 4) the attainment of buddhahood. The unifying theme of all these endeavors is to help all sentient beings proceed along the bodhisattva path so that they too may attain final buddhahood. All beings have the poten-tial to arouse bodhichitta, which would allow them to work consciously on the bodhisattva path and create buddha fields. This in turn allows others to attain buddhahood as well. We can imagine how this simple but potent idea appealed greatly to the uncomplicated peasant mind of east Asia where Pure Land Buddhism distinguished itself as a religion of the masses.

Develop a mind that functions freely, without depending on anything what-soever: This stanza, or a Chinese variation of it, is said to have been the phrase that propelled the young Hui-neng, later the sixth patriarch of Zen, to a spontaneous awakening. It is a rephrasing of the teaching of shunyata: all things are ephemeral, and a well-trained mind should not be mistak-en about the transparent nature of what is seen, heard, smelt, tasted, touched, and thought about. It is a statement about the culmination of the path of the bodhisattva: although the bodhisattva chooses to stay in samsara, she or he is not seduced by the things of samsara and thus dwells in nirvana, free from any kind of clinging. It echoes the Buddha's injunc-tion that the practitioner abide in complete mindfulness, "not clinging to anything in the world."[71]

SECTION 11

The Buddha continued, "Subhuti, what do you think? If someone were to have a body as large as Mount Sumeru, would not this body be very large?"

Subhuti said, "Very large indeed, World-Honored One. Why? Because the Buddha teaches that that which is no-body is known as a large body."

"Subhuti, what do you think? If there were as many Ganges Rivers as there are grains of sand in the Ganges, would the number of grains of sand in all those rivers would be many?"

Subhuti said, "Very many, indeed, World-Honored One. Those Ganges Rivers would indeed be many, much more so the grains of sand in them."

"Subhuti, what do you think? If there were a good man or woman who filled the three thousand chiliocosms containing as many world systems as there are grains of sand in those Ganges Rivers with the seven precious treasures and then gave them all away out of generosity, would not this merit be very great?"

Subhuti said, "Very great, indeed, World-Honored One."

The Buddha said, "I declare to you, Subhuti, if a good man or woman were to accept, practice, and explain even four lines of this sutra to others, such merit would be far greater than the preceding one."

A body as large as Mount Sumeru...: This section initiates a rhetorical endgame in which the Buddha takes Subhuti through a series of inconceivable scenarios in order to reiterate what has already been established: that the preaching of even a stanza from this sutra would accrue more merit than the giving of all material goods.

Mount Sumeru here refers to the "world mountain" that stands at the center of the universe—the *axis mundi* of traditional Buddhist cosmology. The belief in this place is common to Jains, Hindus, and Buddhists. In all religious traditions of east and north Asia, Buddhist and non-Buddhist alike, mountains have often been seen as sacred or polymorphous spaces capable of containing different energies in one place. They have been objects of manifold expressions of appreciation, from religion to poetry to arts. Because of their relative inaccessibility, they have often been referred to as "abodes of gods." In Asia, ascetics who practice in the mountains are especially revered for their endeavors; the mountains are seen as places of purification and power, as "energy points" where it is particularly conducive for the practitioner to meditate.

In folk belief, Mount Kailash, on the present Nepali-Tibetan border, has long been identified as the mythical Mount Sumeru, also known as Mount Meru. In the Buddhist conception Mount Sumeru is surrounded by seas and continents; on its four slopes are the lower and the heavenly abodes.

SECTION 12

"Moreover, Subhuti, wherever this sutra or even four lines of it are preached, that place will be respected by all beings including devas, ashuras, etc., as if it were the Buddha's own chaitya. How much more [worthy of respect] the person who can memorize and recite this sutra [for the benefit of others]! Subhuti, you should know that such a person achieves the highest, foremost, and most

wonderful blessing. Wherever this sutra is kept, the place is to be regarded as if the Buddha or a venerable disciple of his were present."

Continuing the discussion of the superiority of teaching even one stanza of this sutra, the Buddha says that even the places where the sutra is taught will be consecrated. Sacred places have a long ancestry in India—the India of the Buddha's time was dotted with numerous shrines and stupas or reliquary mounds. These places of worship grew out of the pre-Buddhist religious tradition of worshipping trees, tree spirits, serpents, and fertility goddesses. Buddhists adapted this tradition to suit their own purposes. In the mythic accounts of the life of the Buddha, Queen Maya gave birth to her son under a tree; the Buddha gained awakening under the Bodhi Tree and later entered parinirvana while lying between two *sala* trees. The veneration of trees most likely dates from the Indus Valley fertility cults; sacred trees were, and still are, the axis of the religious life of each village in India. Buddhists transferred the patterns of worship that had developed around trees to the cult of the Bodhi Tree. In the cult's most rudimentary form there was an altar at the base of the sacred tree, made out of wood or stone, on which passers-by could leave offerings.

At its most refined, the stupa had many functions. It was a reliquary containing the ashes of the Buddha or of a Buddhist saint; it was a memorial marking the location of a significant event; it was also an architectural embodiment of the Dharma. King Ashoka built stupas at places associated with the birth, the awakening, the teaching of the First Sermon, and the passing away of Shakyamuni Buddha. The remains of these stupas are still to be found in India. Shrines and stupas became meeting places for people of all spiritual persuasions. Here discussions and debates, sometimes acrimonious, other times more tolerant, took place. These debates were the ancient Indian version of town hall meetings in New England, which were crucibles of the democratic experience in America.

In this passage in the *Diamond Sutra*, sacred places are most likely meant when the Buddha discusses locations accorded respect for having the sutra preached there. Prajnaparamita texts proclaimed themselves to be superior to and a substitute for earlier forms of worship, including the stupas:

Other texts, like much of the early Perfection of Wisdom (prajnaparamita) corpus, would proclaim their superiority to stupas, declaring themselves to be substitutes for the body and speech of the absent Buddha, equally worthy of veneration and equally efficacious.[72]

How much more [worthy of respect] the person who can memorize and recite this sutra…: If the preaching and explaining of just four lines from the sutra has the power to consecrate a physical space, how much greater the blessing for the person who can memorize and recite and explain to others the entire sutra! We noted earlier that by the time of the composition of the *Diamond Sutra*, the corporate model of the order was well entrenched, with a group of monks specializing in the memorization and chanting of certain groupings of sutras. This passage, repeated several times throughout the sutra, exhorting the monks to give priority to this sutra over others, is consistent with the intra-Mahayana developments of sutra worship.

The Buddha goes on to say that the place where a copy of the sutra is kept is to be venerated as if the Buddha himself or one of his enlightened disciples were present. The value of a written sutra in ancient India cannot be exaggerated (this is perhaps true of religious texts in all traditions before the invention of movable type). A monk or a nun (or in east Asia, a lay person) would possibly have taken years to copy a sutra from a master copy at the temple. It was a labor of love and devotion. This copy of the sutra would have been his or her most important possession—an object of devotion and inspiration, and a trusted guide on the path of awakening.

SECTION 13

At that time Subhuti said to the Buddha, "World-Honored One, what will this sutra be called? How should we keep its teachings in mind?"

The Buddha said to Subhuti, "This sutra will be called the Vajrachedika Prajnaparamita, The Diamond-Cutter Wisdom That Has Gone Beyond, *because it has the capacity to cut through illusions and afflictions and bring us to the shore of awakening, and by this title you will know it."*

Conze has suggested that this section marks the formal ending of what he considers to be the first part of the sutra and the beginning of a second part. His opinion is that most of the second part of the sutra is actually a medley of misplaced textual and commentarial inserts. He believes that

...reciters at various times added a passage here or there, and that, what is more, the scribes at one time misplaced some of the palm leaves, and also added glosses from the margin into the text. In that case the sequence of the argument would be determined by a series of mechanical accidents.[73]

Certainly there is enough thematic repetition in the second half of the sutra to justify Conze's misgivings. At the same time, the sixteenth-century Chinese Zen monk, Han Shan of the Ming dynasty, in a more evangelically inspired commentary on the *Diamond Sutra*, is of the opinion that the sutra

...has only two parts, Part I dealing with the coarse views held by Subhuti and in fact by all students of Mahayana Buddhism, and Part II dealing with the subtle views still held by them but imperceptible to them.[74]

In other words, according to Han Shan, the repetitions in the second part are concerned with deconstructing the subtle views or intellectualizations not resolved or "uprooted" by the teachings contained in the first part. Whatever the case may be, we can do no more than be on the lookout for teachings not articulated in the first half, while remaining alert to further refinements of previously stated teachings. General, however, the following themes are repeated in different sections:

In section 13 the reference to Prajnaparamita not being Prajnaparamita is a repetition of the discussion in section 7 about Dharma being no-Dharma. The reference to Tathagata having nothing to teach is also a repetition of section 7.

The discussion in section 13 of the negation of dust particles and the chiliocosms is a repetition of the teachings in section 11, as is the reference to the renunciation by sons and daughters of good family (kulaputras). The negation of the thirty-two bodily marks is a reference to the discussion in section 5.

Section 15 is a repetition of the teachings discussed in sections 8, 11, and 12.

In section 16 the reiteration of the incomparable merit resulting from preaching this sutra continues from sections 8, 11, 12, and 15.

In section 17 the first paragraph is a repeat of section 2; the second and third paragraphs are repeats of section 3; while the fourth paragraph is a repeat of section 10. Paragraph 6 is a repeat of section 8; then in the seventh paragraph the sutra veers again toward section 3. In the eighth paragraph the sutra repeats section 10.

Section 19 is a repeat of teachings presented in sections 8, 11, 12, and 15.

Section 20 is a repeat of sections 5 and 13.

The first paragraph in section 21 is a repeat of section 6, and the second paragraph is a repeat of section 14.

Section 24 is a restatement of section 15.

The first few lines of section 25 are a restatement of the teachings expounded earlier in section 3.

Section 28 is a restatement of the teachings put forward earlier in section 4.

Section 30 is essentially a restatement of the teachings contained in the second part of section 13.

Section 31 a recapitulation of what was discussed earlier in section 6.

The first part of section 32 is a restatement of the teachings contained in section 8.

The following list, after Conze, is a guide to the sutra according to topic:

The path of the bodhisattva
1. The vow of a bodhisattva (sections 3, 17)
2. The practice of Perfections (4, 17)
3. Buddhahood and its thirty-two marks (5)
4. Dharmakaya as a body of teachings (6)
5. Dharmakaya as the result of gnosis (7, 17)
6. Dharmakaya as the result of merit (8, 17)

The range of the spiritual life
7. Four stages of sainthood (9)
8. Bodhichitta (10, 17)
9. The bodhisattva and the buddha land (10, 17)
10. The bodhisattva's final nirvana (10, 17)
11. The merit derived from Perfection of Wisdom (11, 12)

Transcendence
12. The dialectical nature of reality (13)
13. The supreme excellence of this teaching (14)
14. Selfless patience and perfect inner freedom (14)
15. Existence and non-existence of beings (14)
16. Truth and falsehood (14, 17)
17. Merit: its acquisition, its presupposition, and its results (14, 15, 16)

The Buddhas
18. The Buddha's five eyes (18)
19. The Buddha's superknowledge (18)
20. The Buddha's merit as no merit (19, 25)
21. The Buddha's physical body (20)
22. The Buddha's teaching (21, 22, 23)
23. The Buddha as healer (25)
24. True nature of a Buddha (26)
25. Effectiveness of meritorious deeds (27, 28, 29)

The material world
26. Views and attitudes (30, 31)
27. Key to true knowledge of the world (32)

In the following sections, therefore, when no commentary is appended, it is to be understood that the theme or themes in that section are a repeat of earlier discussions, as noted above.

To continue section 13:
"And why? The reason is, Subhuti, that what the Tathagata has called the Prajnaparamita, the highest, transcendental wisdom, is not, in fact, the Prajnaparamita and therefore it is called Prajnaparamita.

"Subhuti, what do you think? Is there any Dharma that the Tathagata has taught?"

"No, indeed, World-Honored One, there is none."

"What do you think, Subhuti? Are there many dust particles in the three thousand chiliocosms?"

"Yes, very many, indeed, World-Honored One."

"Subhuti, the Tathagata teaches that what are called dust particles are not dust particles. That is why they are merely dust particles. And what the Tathagata calls chiliocosms are not chiliocosms. That is why they are merely chiliocosms.

"What do you think, Subhuti? Can the Tathagata be recognized through the thirty-two marks [of a great man]?"

"No, World-Honored One, he cannot be recognized through the thirty-two marks. And why? Because the Tathagata has taught that what are called the thirty-two marks are really no-marks. Therefore they are called the thirty-two marks."

"Subhuti, suppose a man or a woman were to renounce all his or her belongings as many times as there are grains of sands in the river Ganges, the merit

thus gained would not exceed that of one who, memorizing even one gatha of four lines of this sutra, preaches them to others."

SECTION 14

Venerable Subhuti, listening to this discourse, through the shock of the Doctrine, had a deep understanding of the meaning of the sutra and was moved to tears. He said to the Buddha, "It is wonderful, indeed, World-Honored One, how well the Tathagata has taught this discourse on Dharma. Through it [a new level of] cognition has been produced in me. Never before have I heard such a discourse on Dharma. World-Honored One, if someone hears this sutra and has pure and clear confidence in it, that person will gain true perception. And what is called true perception is indeed no-perception. This is what the Tathagata teaches as true perception.

"World-Honored One, it is not difficult for me to have faith in, to understand, and to memorize this sutra, which I have just heard. But in the ages to come, in the next five hundred years, if there are beings who, listening to this sutra, are able to believe, understand, and memorize it, they will indeed be most wonderful beings. In them no perception of a self, a person, a being, or a living soul will take place. And why? Because that which is perception of self is no-perception. That which is perception of a being, a person, or a living soul is no-perception. And why? Because the Buddhas have left all perceptions behind."

The Buddha said to Subhuti, "It is just as you say. If there is a person who, listening to this sutra, is not frightened, alarmed, or disturbed, you should know him as a wonderful person. Why? Because what the Tathagata has taught as paramaparamita, the highest perfection, is not the highest perfection and is therefore called the highest perfection.

"Moreover, Subhuti, the teaching of the Tathagata on the perfection of patience is really no perfection and therefore it is the perfection of patience. Why? Subhuti, when, in ancient times, my body was cut to pieces by the king of Kalinga, I did not have the idea of a self, a person, a being, or a living soul. Why? When at that time my body was dismembered limb after limb, joint after joint, feelings of anger and ill will would have arisen in me had I had the idea of a self, a person, a being, or a living soul.

"With my superknowledge I recall that in my past five hundred lifetimes I have led the life of a sage devoted to patience and during those times I did not have the idea of an ego, a person, a being, or a soul.

"Therefore, Subhuti, a bodhisattva, detaching him- or herself from all ideas, should rouse the desire for utmost, supreme, and perfect awakening. He or she

should produce thoughts that are unsupported by forms, sounds, smells, tastes, tangible objects, or mind objects, unsupported by Dharma, unsupported by no-Dharma, unsupported by everything. And why? Because all supports are no supports. This is the reason why the Buddha teaches that a bodhisattva should practice generosity without dwelling on form. Subhuti, the reason he practices generosity is to benefit all beings.

"The Tathagata teaches that all ideas are no-ideas and that all beings are no-beings. Subhuti, the Tathagata is one who speaks of things as they are, speaks what is true, and speaks in accordance with reality. He does not speak deceptively or to please people. Subhuti, in the Dharma attained by the Tathagata there is neither truth nor falsehood.

"Subhuti, if a bodhisattva should practice generosity while still depending on form, he or she is like someone walking in the dark. He or she will not see anything. But when a bodhisattva practices generosity without depending on form, he or she is like someone with good eyesight walking in the bright sunshine—he or she can see all shapes and colors.

"Subhuti, if in times to come the sons and daughters of good families memorize and recite this sutra, they will be seen and recognized by the Tathagata with his buddha knowledge, and they will all acquire immeasurable and infinite merit."

This section continues to focus on deconstructing dualistic categories that have been set up in earlier sections. This is the crux of the sutra: to understand, on one hand, that each named category is a linguistic, intellectual convention that, on investigation, yields no corresponding reality; and to intuit, on the other hand, in one's practice, a middle way between affirming a set of terms (such as perception, self, Dharma, and perfection) and negating another set of terms (such as no-perception, no-self, no-Dharma, and no-perfection). The challenge of the middle way is that it is not something that operates on conventional linguistic and conceptual categories, rather it is a vibrant intellectual and emotional discovery sustaining one's endeavors on the bodhisattva path. This is the ultimate challenge of Buddha's insights: to practice compassion and generosity without getting caught in, and identifying with, what one sees, hears, smells, tastes, touches, or thinks.

Venerable Subhuti…was moved to tears: This phrase is somewhat problematic: arhats are not supposed to be moved to tears. Mahayana asserts that the level of understanding of the highest class of bodhisattvas, of which Subhuti is one, is superior to that of the arhats. The arhats and the highest class of bodhisattvas have supposedly gone beyond the emotions that produce tears. Schopen translates the term *dharmapravegena* as "through the shock of the Doctrine" and argues that this "emotively" charged experience is the only "religious" experience in the sutra. He goes on to say that this experience "may in fact be a prototype and paradigm for at least certain strands of the later Buddhist tradition."[75]

The most reasonable hypothesis here is that Subhuti attained a deeper level of understanding than ever before on hearing this teaching and was filled with gratitude. Schopen's argument is well taken, however, if we compare Subhuti's epiphany with the "sudden awakening" experiences of the Zen tradition. Whether these experiences are facilitated by mundane events of daily life or passages from a sutra (we have evidence for both), they translate experientially into a shock of recognition that the truth was always there but obscured by filters or clouds of one's own delusions.

Never before have I heard such a discourse...: The hypothesis above seems to be confirmed by Subhuti saying here that even with the wisdom eye acquired by him in his previous lives, he has never heard such a lucid teaching on the wisdom perfection or prajnaparamita.

Because the Buddhas have left all perceptions behind: The Buddhas are those who have transcended false perceptions and their attendant illusions (created by the notions of I, mine, and me) and are able to rest completely in things just as they are—in the suchness of things. This suchness is nirvana.

The well-known opening lines of the classical poem *Hsin Shin Ming* (Faith Mind Verse) by the third Zen patriarch Seng T'san,

> The Great Way is not difficult
> for those who have no [addiction to] preferences

are an eloquent confirmation of this teaching from the *Diamond Sutra.* The middle way of the Buddha is the "great" way because through it one transcends one's habitual way of responding to the phenomenal world with clinging or aversion. Accepting the suchness of the phenomenal world wholeheartedly, without addiction to clinging or aversion—or to suchness itself—is entering into nirvana, the state of awakening, which is liberation from all attachment.

Not frightened, alarmed, or disturbed...: The Buddha states that those who are not frightened or disturbed by these teachings will be truly blessed. Across a gulf of nearly two thousand years we can see the acuity of this insight—human thinking remains addicted to categorical affirmation or denial. Our dualistic thinking continues to be the source of our greatest confusion, both personal and collective. A Buddha is a Buddha through freedom from views, from the need to affirm or deny all that is in the realm of the relative, all that is supported by linguistic conventions, but not by reality.

The perfection of patience: Having established a broad framework for looking at the world through the prism of shunyata, the sutra here talks about the perfection of patience. It introduces a new subject and seeks to provide a balance between the absolute and the relative. The stratosphere of shunyata is rarefied indeed and not always easy to breathe in. But within that framework there is still the need to find some modus operandi of living in the world of the relative. What are the guidelines, if any? The answer in the *Diamond Sutra* is the perfections.

We must keep in mind that the perfections discussed in the Buddhist tradition are not moral injunctions one adopts as rewards or punishments. They work on the existential as well as the cosmological level. On the existential level, one can immediately experience the fruit of a wholesome or unwholesome engagement (through thought, speech, and action) in one's own mind-body system. When one is engaged in unwholesome conduct, on the one hand, one experiences a contraction or stress, a sense of something impinging on one's mind-body system. On the other hand, wholesome conduct produces a feeling of expansion, of spaciousness, of being at peace with oneself and with the universe.

In this section, the Buddha reiterates the power that comes from cultivating wholesome engagements over many lifetimes. He refers to one of his previous lives when he was an ascetic in the forest. The king of Kalinga had gone into the forest on a hunting expedition accompanied by several concubines. While the men in the party were out hunting, the women went exploring in the forest and found the ascetic sitting in meditation surrounded by an aura of tremendous peace. When the hunting party returned, the king went looking for his mistresses and found them sitting at the feet of the ascetic in a state of enchantment. In a fit of jealousy, the king ordered each of the ascetic's limbs to be cut off, one after the other. In the face of this violence to his body, the ascetic only said "patience," even as each of his limbs was cut off.

The Buddha goes on to say that it would not have been possible for him to have been so firmly grounded in the perfection of patience had he had any idea of an ego-self, a person, a living being, or a soul. Thus the implication is that the practice of each of these perfections (wholesome conduct, kindness, patience, effort, meditation, and wisdom) is truly possible only when one simultaneously develops the perfection of wisdom, of shunyata, by relinquishing the idea of someone who is practicing these perfections in a proprietary sense. This is the central theme of the *Diamond Sutra:* in the practice of perfections there is no sense of gain or loss.

The practice of the perfections without a proprietary sense of self is the core organizing principle of the bodhisattva path and leads to the creation of buddha fields where the bodhisattva, now become a Buddha, welcomes all beings to the pure land so that they are, in turn, empowered to walk the bodhisattva path, create buddha fields, become Buddhas, and thus continue to work for the awakening of all beings.

In this section of the *Diamond Sutra* the Buddha goes on to say that he devoted himself to the cultivation of the perfection of patience not only when his limbs were cut off one by one, but over five hundred lifetimes. And in all those lives he was not distracted by the idea of an ego-self, a person, a living being, or a soul.

The story of Buddha's limbs being cut off may appear irrelevant or unnecessarily gruesome to Western practitioners, but it might help to remember that 1) in traditional societies shamans commonly experience metaphorical dismemberment when they embark on visionary journeys in that they actually feel the pain of the experience in their body; and 2) for meditators on a long retreat, experiences of "psychological dismemberment" are not uncommon. Seeing through the illusion of ego and consequently losing the habitual structure of the self are traumatic, "dismembering" experiences for many, which may express themselves through pains in the body. More than anything else, this story may highlight the disdain or indifference held by the yogic-shamanic traditions for the corporeal body, which is seen merely as a readily available tool for accessing whatever the adept is seeking.

The reason he practices generosity is to benefit all beings: Paradoxical as it may seem, the Buddha says that a bodhisattva should practice generosity in order to benefit all beings, and yet there are no beings in the absolute sense. All practices and all benefits, therefore, exist only in the realm of the relative, hence are only skillful means.

All ideas are no-ideas and...all beings are no-beings: As we see again and again throughout the sutra, "ideas" and "beings" are dualistic categories, operational only in the realm of the relative. They have no essence of their own. Their matrix is shunyata, out of which they emerge and into which they return. Hence, in truth, they are no-ideas and no-beings, and yet they do appear. The challenge is to not become attached to the notion of no-ideas or no-beings.

The Tathagata is one who speaks of things as they are: The Tathagata is not seeking approval of his (or her) ideas from others. The Tathagata has seen the momentary appearances of things in the phenomenal world over unimaginably long eons and has seen that appearances are without essence or true existence of their own.

In the Dharma attained by the Tathagata there is neither truth nor falsehood: Truth and falsehood both belong to the realm of the relative and are therefore conceptual categories. The Tathagata speaks not of conceptual categories but of direct perception into the nature of things. The Tathagata is not trying to please anyone. The Tathagata is the embodiment of the experience of the unconditioned, which is beyond predication—it is not subject to the linguistic notions of truth or falsehood.

Section 15

"Furthermore, Subhuti, if one should renounce in the morning all one's belongings as many times as there are grains of sand in the River Ganges, and if one should do likewise at noon and in the evening and continue thus for countless ages; and if someone else, on hearing this discourse on Dharma, were to accept it with a believing heart, the merit acquired by the latter would far exceed that of the former. How much more the merit of one who would copy, memorize, learn, recite, and expound it for others!

"Subhuti, to sum up, immeasurable, innumerable, and incomprehensible is this discourse on Dharma. The Tathagata has taught it for the well-being of those who have set out in the best, in the most excellent vehicle. Those who take up this discourse on Dharma, bear it in mind, recite, study, and expound it in detail for others will all be known to the Tathagata and recognized by him and acquire merit that is incomparable, measureless, and infinite. Such beings will share in the supreme awakening attained by the Tathagata. Why? Because, Subhuti, this course on the Dharma could not be understood by beings of inferior resolve, nor by those attached to the idea of a self, a person, a being, or a living soul. [Being so caught up], they are unable to hear, memorize, learn, recite, and expound this sutra.

"Moreover, Subhuti, the spot of earth where this sutra will be revealed, that spot of earth will be worthy of worship by the whole world with its gods, men, ashuras, worthy of being saluted respectfully, worthy of being honored by circumambulation. That spot of earth will be like a shrine or temple."

Section 16

"And yet Subhuti, there will be some sons and daughters of good families who will be despised for their memorizing and reciting of this sutra. This is due to their previous evil karma. The impure deeds that these beings have done in their former lives are liable to lead them into states of woe in this lifetime. But [if they are not averse to] being despised in the present life, whatever evil karma they produced in their previous lives will be destroyed, and they will be able to attain the awakening of a Buddha.

"Subhuti, with my superknowledge, I recall that in the past, even before I was with Dipankara Buddha, I made offerings, and had been attendant, to eighty-four thousand multi-million Buddhas. But the merit I gained from that service is not one hundredth nor even one hundredth million of the merit of someone who, at the time of the collapse of the Dharma, memorizes, recites, and learns from this sutra and expound it to others. It bears neither number, nor fraction, nor enumeration, nor similarity, nor comparison, nor resemblance.

"Moreover, Subhuti, the merit acquired by good men and women who, at the time of the collapse of the Dharma, memorize, recite, and learn this sutra will be so great that if I were to describe it in detail, some people would become suspicious and disbelieving, and their minds might become disoriented. Subhuti, you should know that the meaning of this sutra is beyond comprehension and discussion. Likewise, the fruit that results from receiving and practicing this sutra is beyond comprehension and discussion."

The sectarian fervor of the Mahayana sutras can again be discerned in this section. The sutra is exhorting adherents not to be discouraged by criticism from others for having faith in the teachings of the sutra. It suggests that unwholesome actions in past lives are the karmic cause of their being reviled by their foes. If they remain steadfast in their faith in the sutra, the fruits of this faith will be theirs, beyond verbal comprehension and discussion. We can surmise from this section that, in addition to opposition from the non-Buddhist religions, sectarian rivalries may have been present within the Buddhist sangha during the time of the composition of the sutra.

Section 17

At that time, the Venerable Subhuti said to the Buddha, "World-Honored One, may I ask you again? If the sons and daughters of good family wish to arouse the thought of supreme enlightenment, how should they abide in it? How should they keep their thought under control?"

The Buddha replied, "Someone who has set out on the bodhisattva path should cherish one thought only: 'When I attain perfect wisdom, I will liberate all sentient beings in every realm of the universe, whether they be egg-born, womb-born, moisture-born, miraculously born; those with form, those without form, those with perception, those without perception, and those with neither perception nor non-perception so long as any form of being is conceived, I must allow it to pass into the eternal peace of nirvana, into that realm of nirvana that leaves nothing behind, and to attain final awakening."

"And yet, although immeasurable, innumerable, and unlimited beings have been liberated, truly no being has been liberated. Why, Subhuti? Because if a bodhisattva entertains such thoughts as a self, a person, a being, or a living soul, he is not a true bodhisattva.

"Subhuti, in fact, there is no independently existing object of mind called the supreme, perfect awakening. What do you think, Subhuti? In ancient times, when the Tathagata was living with Dipankara Buddha, did he attain anything called the supreme, perfect awakening?"

"No, World-Honored One. According to what I understand, there is no attainment of anything called the supreme, perfect awakening."

The Buddha said, "Right you are! It is for this reason that the Dipankara Buddha then predicted of me: 'You, young Brahmin, will be in a future time a Tathagata, an arhat, fully enlightened, by the name of Shakyamuni!' This prediction was made because there is, in fact, nothing that can be attained that is called the supreme, perfect awakening.

"Why is this? Because, Subhuti, 'Tathagata' is synonymous with true suchness (tathata) of all dharmas. And if someone were to say, 'The Tathagata has fully known the utmost, right, and perfect liberation,' he would be speaking falsely. Why? Because there is no Dharma by which the Tathagata has fully known the utmost, right, and perfect awakening. And the Dharma that the Tathagata has fully known and demonstrated is neither graspable nor elusive. Therefore the Tathagata teaches 'All dharmas are the Buddha's own and special Dharmas.' Why? All dharmas, Subhuti, have been taught by the Tathagata as no-dharmas. Therefore all dharmas are expediently called the Buddha's own and special Dharmas.

"Subhuti, a comparison can be made with the idea of a great human body. What the Tathagata calls a great body is in fact a no-body. So it is, Subhuti, with the bodhisattvas. If a bodhisattva were to think, 'I will lead all beings to nirvana,' he or she should not be considered a bodhisattva. Why? Because there

is no such thing as a 'bodhi being' (bodhi sattva). It is because of this that the Tathagata teaches that all dharmas are without the notion of a self, a person, a being, or a living soul.

"Subhuti, furthermore, if a bodhisattva were to say, 'I will create harmonious buddha fields,' he or she likewise should not be called a bodhi being. Why? The Tathagata has taught that the harmonious buddha fields are not in fact harmonious buddha fields. Such is merely a name. It is thus that he speaks of truly harmonious buddha fields.

"Subhuti, a bodhisattva who thoroughly understands the principle of no-self and no-dharma as the true self and the true Dharma [respectively] is to be considered an authentic bodhisattva."

"All dharmas are the Buddha's own and special Dharmas": The teaching of the Tathagata, the fully awakened Buddha, is that all dharmas are no-dharmas; when taught by the Tathagata, these no-dharmas are the true Dharma and therefore the Buddha's special Dharma. This linguistic play is designed to get across the idea, once again, that the teachings of the Tathagata are skillful means and are not to be appropriated as an ideology. The same linguistic analogue is presented at the end of the section when no-self is equated with the true self, and no-dharma with the true Dharma.

The teaching of no-self or anatman has been the subject of endless debate both within and outside of Buddhism. The greatest problems have arisen when either proponents or opponents have treated this teaching as a metaphysical statement. In Buddha's teachings, both in the Pali sutras and the Prajnaparamita tradition, the teaching of no-self is a therapeutic device. The Buddha responded to the Brahminical formulation of a permanent entity, the self or atman, with silence, without taking a position either for or against. Had he taken a position, he would have produced an alternate concept, which would not have been in keeping with the framework of his teaching.

The Buddha gave primacy to personal experience. Direct perception into one's own experience allows a practitioner to become free of the concepts of self or no-self, dharmas or no-dharmas. This awareness or direct perception has meant, for practitioners, an expansion of self-imposed boundaries of "self" and a merging, so to speak, with the true or universal self. It cannot be cautioned too often that in pure experience, linguistic terms do not suffice. The Buddha also gives this warning in this passage.

The dissolution of the limited self through direct perception into the nature of phenomena and the expansion of the field of awareness pertains to the holographic model we discussed earlier. On the one hand, one lets go of the notion of a particularized self and, on the other, one lets go of any clinging to views. There is thus no distinction between one's being and one's views. The later Zen tradition captures this fusion of one's being and one's views as no-thought or not-knowing. The well-known lines from Zen master Dogen speak to this fusion:

> Studying the Buddha Way is studying oneself;
> Studying oneself is forgetting oneself;
> Forgetting oneself is being enlightened by all things;
> Being enlightened by all things is causing the body-mind
> of oneself and the body-mind of others to be shed.[76]

SECTION 18

"Subhuti, what do you think? Does the Tathagata possess the human eye?"
  Subhuti replied, "Yes, World-Honored One, he does."
  "Subhuti, what do you think? Does the Tathagata possess the divine eye?"
  "Yes, World-Honored One, he does."
  "Subhuti, what do you think? Does the Tathagata possess the gnostic eye?"
  "Yes, World-Honored One, he does."
  "Subhuti, what do you think? Does the Tathagata possess the prajna eye?"
  "Yes, World-Honored One, he does."
  "Subhuti, what do you think? Does the Tathagata possess the buddha eye?"
  "Yes, World-Honored One, he does."
  "Subhuti, what do you think? Has the Tathagata taught about the grains of sand in the Ganges River?"
  "Yes, World-Honored One, he has."
  "Subhuti, what do you think? If there were as many Ganges Rivers as there are grains of sand in the Ganges River and if there were a buddha land for each one of those grains of sand, would those buddha lands be many?"
  "Yes, World-Honored One, they would be many indeed."
  "Subhuti, I declare to you that however many living beings there may be in all of these manifold buddha lands and though each one of them has numerous trends of thought, the Tathagata has known them all. How is it so? Because the Tathagata teaches that all trends of thought are actually not trends of thought, and that is why he calls them trends of thought. Why? Because the past mind cannot be gotten hold of, the future mind cannot be gotten hold of, and the present mind cannot be gotten hold of."

In the first section the Buddha goes through a hierarchy to establish the levels of "seeing into the nature of things"—the human eye, the divine eye, the gnostic eye, the prajna eye, and the buddha eye. With the human eye one sees the flowers, the sky, and the clouds. The divine eye sees things regardless of the obstacles of time and space. This is the eye of the "gods" living in the god realms and of the clairvoyant seer. The gnostic or "insight" eye allows one to see the impermanence and lack of self-nature in all living beings. This is the eye of the hearers and solitary awakened ones; although these practitioners have awakened to the truth they do not yet have the full awakening of a Tathagata.

The prajna eye is the eye of transcendent wisdom that enables bodhisattvas to see the empty nature of all phenomena. Thich Nhat Hanh contends that this is the eye

> ...that can see the true nature of the emptiness of all objects of mind. It can see the nature of awakened mind and of the great vow. A bodhisattva with the eye of transcendent wisdom sees that he or she and all beings share the same nature of emptiness...[77]

The buddha eye is the eye of the Tathagata with which he or she sees the past, the present, and the future as well as the minds of all beings in the past, the present, and the future. We may recall that this is one of the superknowledges said to have been acquired by Siddhartha Gautama during the night of his awakening under the bodhi tree and part of his becoming the Buddha, the Tathagata, the fully enlightened one.

Nothing in the universe is hidden from the buddha eye. And, having seen everything with the buddha eye, the Tathagata knows that there is no place where the past, the present, or the future "mind," so to speak, can be found. As mentioned earlier, this is the famous line with which the tea-lady stumped Te-shan and facilitated his progress as a future great Ch'an master.

SECTION 19

"What do you think, Subhuti? If a son or daughter of good family were to fill the three thousand chiliocosms with the seven precious treasures and then give them as a gift to the Tathagatas, the arhats, the fully enlightened ones, would the merit of that act be great?"

Subhuti replied, "Yes, it would be great indeed, O Lord."

The Buddha said, "So it is, Subhuti, so it is. But if, in reality, there were such a thing as a great heap of merit, the Tathagata would not have spoken of it as a great heap of merit. Such is merely a name. It is because it is without a foundation that the Tathagata has spoken of it as a great heap of merit."

Because it is without a foundation: This is a reassertion of the earlier teaching that things in the phenomenal world do not have a self-nature or an own-being; as such they exist relative to the time during which the phenomenon holds its form. It is to be understood that when the Tathagata speaks of the heap of merit, he is speaking of the world of relativity and conditionality rather than of an absolute world where it would be impossible to speak of merit as such.

SECTION 20

"What do you think, Subhuti? Can the Tathagata be seen by means of his perfectly formed body?"

Subhuti said, "No, World-Honored One. As I understand it, the Tathagata is not to be seen by means of his perfectly formed body. Why? Because the Tathagata has taught that what is called a perfectly formed body is not a perfectly formed body. Such is merely a name. Therefore it is called a perfectly formed body."

The Buddha asked further, "What do you think, Subhuti? Can the Tathagata be seen by means of his possession of bodily marks?"

Subhuti replied, "No, World-Honored One. As I understand it, the Tathagata cannot be by means of his possession of the bodily marks. Why? Because the Tathagata has taught that what are called the bodily marks are not in fact bodily marks. Such is merely a name. Therefore they are called the bodily marks."

Such is merely a name: Bodily form and the marks of the Buddha, no matter how perfectly formed they may be, cannot contain the living, boundless reality that is the Tathagata. The reference to bodily form and marks in a conventional sense may point to the reality but cannot contain it. The conventional way of talking about it is merely a name.

SECTION 21

The Buddha asked, "What do you think, Subhuti? Does the Tathagata think, 'I have taught the Dharma'? Subhuti, whosoever says that the Tathagata thinks this way slanders the Tathagata; he would misrepresent me by seizing on what is not there. Why? The Tathagata has taught that in the teaching of the Dharma there is no Dharma that can be pointed to as Dharma. Such is merely a name. That is why it is called the teaching of Dharma."

Subhuti asked, "World-Honored One, will there be beings in the future, five hundred years from now, at the time of the collapse of the Dharma, who will truly believe these teachings?"

The Buddha said, "Subhuti, there are neither beings nor no-beings. Why? The Tathagata has taught that what are called beings are truly no beings. Such is merely a name. That is why the Tathagata has spoken of them as beings."

SECTION 22

"Subhuti, what do you think? Is there any Dharma by [means of] which the Tathagata has understood perfect, unexcelled awakening?"

Subhuti said, "No, World-Honored One. As I understand it, there is no Dharma by which the Tathagata has understood perfect, unexcelled awakening."

The Buddha said, "So it is, Subhuti, so it is. Not even the least trace of Dharma is to be found anywhere. Such is merely a name. That is why it is called the perfect, unexcelled awakening."

The structure of the first part of this section poses a major translation problem. Conze's translation from Sanskrit is radically different from the Chinese translations, followed by Thich Nhat Hanh, A. F. Price, and D. T. Suzuki. In the Chinese-based translations, it is Subhuti who asks the Buddha a question to lead off the section. In Conze's translation Subhuti continues to play the straight man. The Chinese version seems to me an aberration in so far as the structure of the sutra is concerned. For this reason I have chosen to go along with Conze's version.

The perfect, unexcelled awakening (anuttara samyaksambodhi) is the experience of the Buddha in the hour of his full awakening, turning him into the Tathagata. In traditional understanding anuttara samyaksambodhi means accessing the ten powers, discussed earlier, and also encapsulating the hierarchy of human eye, divine eye, gnostic eye, prajna eye, and buddha eye, and the "powers" associated with them.

No Dharma by which the Tathagata has understood...: The intention of these lines is to negate the instrumentality of any dharma in causing anuttara samyaksambodhi. The Buddha here points out that there is no dharma that can be identified with anuttara samyaksambodhi. In the Prajna-paramita tradition, the perfect, unexcelled awakening refers to direct perception into the nature of things rather than to any dharma by or to which one awakens. These powers are still in the realm of the relative and are not the concern of the Tathagata. What is of concern to the Tathagata is the prajna wisdom that sees the lack of self-nature in all things. Both the *Heart Sutra* and the *Diamond Sutra* are saying that awakening cannot be equated with any dharma. Awakening is in the realm of the absolute, while dharmas, as names and designations, are in the realm of the relative.

SECTION 23

"Furthermore, Subhuti, the dharma called the anuttara samyaksambodhi is at one with everything else. Nothing in it is at variance with anything else. That is why it is called the perfect, unexcelled awakening. It is self-identical through the absence of a self, a person, a being, or a living soul, and that is why it is fully known as the totality of all the wholesome dharmas. And yet, Subhuti, no dharmas have been taught by the Tathagata. Such is merely a name. Thus are they called 'wholesome dharmas.'"

This section is a continuation of the discussion from the preceding section. Although the anuttara samyaksambodhi is called a dharma here, it is to be understood that this is a linguistic use only. As an experience, anuttara samyaksambodhi is identical to the absence of all conceptual categories, including dharmas, self, person, being, and living soul. When all conceptual categories are absent, and when one is not deluded by contrary points of view, this is the realm of "wholesome" dharmas, because it is not at odds with anything but is fully inclusive of everything without distinction. This realm can only be experienced and cannot be conceptualized. We may name it, but we must remain cognizant of its limitation as a concept.

SECTION 24

"Again, Subhuti, if a son or daughter of a good family were to pile up the seven precious treasures in the three thousand chiliocosms and give them away as a gift, the merit resulting from such an act would be much less than that of someone who was to memorize but one stanza from this Vajrachedika Prajna-paramita *and teach it to others. The merit of the latter would indeed be so great that no comparison could be made."*

SECTION 25

"Subhuti, you must not think that the Tathagata entertains the notion 'I will bring all living beings to the shore of awakening.' Why? Because in reality there are no beings who can be liberated by the Tathagata. To entertain the notion that there are beings who can be liberated would be to partake in the idea of a self, a person, a being and a living soul. The Tathagata has taught that one must not seize upon these notions, and yet foolish common people have seized upon them. Subhuti, though the Tathagata uses the words 'foolish common people,' in reality there are no such people. Such is merely a name. That is why they are called foolish common people."

SECTION 26

"Subhuti, what do you think? Is the Tathagata to be recognized by means of his possession of [bodily] marks?"

Subhuti replied, "No, World-Honored One."

The Buddha said, "If, Subhuti, the Tathagata could be recognized by means of his possession of [bodily] marks, then the chakravartin also would be a Tathagata. Therefore the Tathagata is not to be recognized by means of his possession of [bodily] marks."

Subhuti said, "As I understand the Tathagata's teaching, he is not to be recognized by means of his [bodily] marks."

Then the Buddha uttered the following stanzas:

> *Those who saw me through my form,*
> *And those who heard me by my voice,*
> *False endeavors they engaged in;*
> *Me those people will not see.*

> *A Buddha is to be seen [known] through dharma[kaya],*
> *And his guidance manifests from dharma[kaya].*
> *Yet the true nature of dharma[kaya] cannot be understood,*
> *And it is not capable of being known.*

In ancient India, the term *chakravartin* (literally, wheel turner) was used to denote a universal monarch. We may recall that in the century immediately preceding the birth of the Buddha tribal oligarchies had been slowly yielding to a new political and military unit of organization—the monarchy. The lifetime of the Buddha was marked by the presence of six-teen major republics and kingdoms in the known parts of India. In this still-evolving social and political environment, a chakravartin was a potent symbol for political ambition and hegemony. He stood for a political ruler who set out to "conquer" the world, that is, bring together the disparate kingdoms and republics under one central political authority. The chakra-vartin was supposed to be born, not made, in the sense that he suppos-edly was born with certain bodily marks. A legend about the life of the Buddha tells us that astrologers found these auspicious marks on the new-born's body and predicted to his father that the boy would become either a great chakravartin or a great sage. In either case he would be a "world conqueror." The legend goes on to describe how the father tried to create an environment that would inspire young Siddhartha to become a chakra-vartin rather than a renouncer.

In this section, the Buddha reminds Subhuti that if it were simply a matter of bodily marks, the chakravartin would be interchangeable with a Tathagata, but a Tathagata transcends mere bodily marks.

The two stanzas the Buddha utters are a poetic recapitulation of this distinction. Those who look for a Tathagata merely by means of bodily marks and cling to physical appearance are simply deluding themselves. They will never be able to discern the true Tathagata, which is the dharma-kaya—the formless, boundless reality underlying all forms. This dharma-kaya is shunyata; the teaching of shunyata by the Tathagata is the expression of the dharmakaya. This Dharma expression is the true guid-ance for all aspirants. Yet the true nature of dharmakaya, being shunyata itself, cannot be discerned and cannot be known as an object. The prajna wisdom teaches that shunyata can only be known as suchness of both the subject and the object. Dharma or shunyata can only be intuited, not known, at least as an object. The last line of the sutra implies a caution against wanting to objectify dharmakaya as something that can be known analytically. At the very least, it cannot be apprehended as an object.

SECTION 27

"Subhuti, you should not think that the Tathagata has attained the anuttara samyaksambodhi by virtue of his possession of the thirty-two [bodily] marks. Why? Because the Tathagata could not have attained the anuttara samyak-sambodhi through possession of [bodily] marks [alone].

"At the same time, Subhuti, no one should say that those who have set out

on the path of the bodhisattva need to see all dharmas in terms of their anni-
hilation. I declare to you, Subhuti, that those who set out in the bodhisattva-
yana do not entertain any notion of the annihilation of dharmas."

In a somewhat jarring turn of phrase, the Buddha says that even though
the Tathagata is not to be recognized or limited to the thirty-two bodily
marks, he is not advocating a nihilistic notion. His statement that the
bodhisattvas should not entertain any ideas of "annihilation of dharmas"
goes to the heart of the Mahayana teaching of suchness.

Historically, it may be that at the time of the composition of the *Dia-*
mond Sutra, the Mahayana was responding to a perception within the larger Indian religious tradition that the sangha was championing a pessimistic
or nihilistic way of looking at the human condition. It may also be, given
the amorphous nature of the Mahayana movement, that there was a branch
of Mahayana that was advocating the necessity of annihilating the dharmas,
and that the *Diamond Sutra* was responding to such a way of thinking.

Through the teachings of the two levels of truth and of suchness, Mahayana advocated seeing things just as they are, without needing to "anni-
hilate" or cling to them. In later articulation, the teaching of suchness goes
even further and says that in their suchness things are perfect and absolute.
While the things of the world are encrusted with defilements in their relative aspect, in their absolute aspect they are pure and untainted. One accepts
the relative truth of appearances, but one discerns that in their absolute
aspect they are permeated with shunyata and thus have no self-nature.

SECTION 28

"Again, Subhuti, if a son or daughter of good family were to fill as many world
systems as there are grains of sands in the Ganges River with the seven precious
treasures and give them as a gift to the Tathagatas, arhats, fully enlightened
ones, and if, on the other hand, a bodhisattva were to gain the insight that all
dharmas are empty and have no self-nature or essence of their own, his or her
merit would be immeasurably and incalculably [greater than that of the for-
mer]. Why is that? Because bodhisattvas are immune to any rewards of merit."

Subhuti asked, "What does it mean, World-Honored One, that the bodhi-
sattvas are immune to rewards of merit?"

The Buddha said, "The bodhisattva whose merit is great does not get caught
in the desire for or idea of merit. She or he understands that such is merely a
name. It is for this reason that the bodhisattva is immune to the rewards of merit."

SECTION 29

"Whosoever says that the Tathagata goes or comes, stands, sits or lies down does not understand the meaning of my teaching. Why? The Tathagata does not come from anywhere, nor does he depart to anywhere. Therefore he is called the Tathagata, the arhat, the fully enlightened one."

This section recapitulates the earlier statement in sections 5 and 20 about the Tathagata being the dharmakaya—the eternal, numinous presence outside the confines of time and space, appearance and disappearance.

SECTION 30

"Subhuti, what do you think? If a son or daughter of good family were to grind as many world systems as there are particles of dust in the three thousand chiliocosms as finely as they can be ground with incalculable vigor, would that be an enormous collection of dust particles?"

Subhuti replied, "Yes, World-Honored One, it would indeed be an enormous collection. Why? If the dust particles had any real self-existence, the Tathagata would not have called them an enormous collection of dust particles. As I understand it, what the Tathagata calls a collection of dust particles is not in essence a collection of dust particles. Such is merely a name. It is for this reason that it is called a collection of dust particles. Moreover, what the Tathagata has taught as the system of three thousand chiliocosms is not in fact a system of chiliocosms. That is why they are called chiliocosms. To consider the chiliocosms as real would be a case of seizing on a material object that is nothing but an assembly of dust particles. That is why it is called seizing on an object."

The Buddha added, "What is called seizing upon a material object is a matter of linguistic convention without factual content. It is not a dharma or a no-dharma. And yet the foolish common people have seized upon it."

SECTION 31

"Subhuti, what do you think? If someone were to say that the Tathagata has taught the view of self, person, being, or living soul, would that person have understood my meaning?"

Subhuti replied, "No, World-Honored One, such a person would not have understood the Tathagata. Why? What the Tathagata calls a self-view, a person-view, a being-view, or a living soul-view are not in essence a self-view, a person-view, a being-view, or a living soul-view. That is why they are called a self-view, a person-view, a being-view, or a living soul-view."

The Buddha said, "It is in this manner, Subhuti, that someone who has set out on the bodhisattva path should know all dharmas, see that all dharmas are like this, and should have confidence in the understanding of all dharmas without any conception of dharmas. Subhuti, what the Tathagata has called a conception of dharmas is not a conception of dharmas. Such is merely a name. That is why it is called a conception of dharmas."

SECTION 32

"Again, Subhuti, if a son or daughter of good family were to pile up the seven precious treasures in all the three thousand chiliocosms and give them away as a gift to the Tathagatas, the arhats, and the fully enlightened ones, and, on the other hand, if someone were to take but one stanza from this Vajrachedika Prajnaparamita *and bear it in mind, teach it, recite and study it, and illuminate it in full detail for others, his or her merit would be much more immeasurable and incalculable [than that of the former]. And in what spirit would he or she illuminate it for others? Without being caught up in the appearances of things in themselves but understanding the nature of things just as they are. Why? Because:*

> *So you should see [view] all of the fleeting world:*
> *A star at dawn, a bubble in the stream;*
> *A flash of lightning in a summer cloud;*
> *A flickering lamp, a phantom, and a dream.*

When the Buddha had finished [speaking], Venerable Subhuti, the monks and nuns, the pious lay men and women, the bodhisattvas, and the whole world with its gods, ashuras, and gandharvas were filled with joy at the teaching, and, taking it to heart, they went their separate ways.

The verse above is my adaptation of A. F. Price's translation from the Chinese. It is much more readable than Conze's more literal translation:

> As stars, a fault of vision,
> as a lamp, mock show, dew drops, or a bubble,
> A dream, a lightning flash, or cloud,
> So should one view what is conditioned.

For once I have chosen to follow the Chinese version. It is more poetic and poignant, and through it the core teaching of the sutra somehow reaches into our hearts in a way that is not possible with a dry, academic translation. Although this verse is not as well known as the *Heart Sutra* mantra *(Gate gate paragate parasamgate bodhi svaha),* it nonetheless captures the urgency that the sutra is trying to convey: the world of appearances is fleeting, ephemeral, transitory, and lacking in self-essence.

If this verse encapsulates the teachings of the *Diamond Sutra*, how are we to understand it in our own time and place? Here we run into issues of fundamental assumptions about life and its meaning in the Buddhist tradition. The core message of the Buddha, configured as the four noble truths, is that human existence is marked by the three characteristics known as dukkha (dis-ease), *anitya* (transitoriness), and anatman (lack of anything worthy of self-identification anywhere in the mind-body system). These fundamental assumptions are open to direct investigation by each one of us in our own experience.

Throughout Buddhist teachings we find this core message (whether attributed directly to the Buddha or to the later commentarial tradition): the world, which we are so eager to appropriate, is merely a play of shadows. This ancient wisdom is not something confined to Buddha's teachings but is an integral part of how the ancients looked at the world. It is present in Plato's famous allegory of the cave. What the Buddha sought through his teachings was to establish a healthy relationship between the self and this fleeting, transitory world. This is the essence of the *Diamond Sutra:* how to view the world around us so that we are not taken in by the mere appearance of things and hence not caught in the suffering that samsara brings. Like all Buddhist scriptures, it teaches a way of being in the world without being of it.

The poignancy of the images evoked in this verse parallels the fragility and transitoriness of our own human existence: *a star at dawn*—faintly seen and just about to disappear; *a bubble in the stream; a flash of lightning*—formed only for an instant and disappearing in the blink of an eye; *a summer cloud*—only seemingly substantial and constantly changing shape; *a flickering lamp*—doomed to restlessness, unable to stabilize enough to have any meaningful identity; *a phantom*—of such chaotic interiority that one cannot be sure of its shape; *a dream*—of such dubious existence that one cannot distinguish what is real and what is not.

The core doctrinal question in the Buddhist tradition, in the face of the teachings of anatman and shunyata, is: what is it that gets transformed?

The resounding response of the *Diamond Sutra*, as encapsulated in its last verse, is that what gets transformed is one's perception or way of looking at the world and at oneself. This transformed view is the wise view or the way of seeing that gives one an efficacious perspective on the conditioned things of the world.

At the time when the *Diamond Sutra* was composed as part of the Prajnaparamita tradition to cultivate the wise view, parallel doctrinal developments were engaged in the same enterprise. Nagarjuna and his followers in the Madhyamaka school had already put forward the theory of two truths—ultimate truth (shunyata) and relative (constructed or conventional) truth. The Yogachara school had refined this doctrine further by proposing the three-nature *(trisvabhava)* theory in which they essentially split the relative truth of the Madhyamaka in two and proposed that what is knowable by the mind *(chitta)* has three aspects: the imaginary, the dependent, and the ultimate. The example that is most often used to illustrate this three-nature theory is that of a mirage of water in the desert. The water is perceived by the traveler as a solid, real object; this is the imaginary aspect. The imagining of water is dependent on the thirst of the traveler. When the traveler reaches the spot where the water was imagined, no water is to be found. This lack of water in the imagined object is the ultimate. What becomes clear through this formulation is that our underlying thirst for having or becoming distorts our perception of reality in ways that allow us to imagine things as solid objects where there is no solidity but only a momentary construction that is the result of interdependent causes and conditions. When we reach out to touch what seemed solid, it turns out to be a mirage, an illusion.

All these three traditions of Mahayana are thus in the service of a wise view that advocates seeing all phenomena as empty, thus allowing clear perception in each moment of encounter with the phenomenal world and also freedom from dukkha that might arise as a result of clinging to an illusion. A complete and thorough understanding derived through wisdom of the nature of conditioned phenomena means that one is able to break free of the hold that these conditioned things normally have over one's consciousness. This freedom is *ipso facto* a state of nirvana.

The Buddhist conception of nirvana is synonymous with complete nonattachment—whether to the events of our own life or the vast cosmic drama being played out around us. Nonattachment is the result of direct insight into the nature of things, both psychological and phenomenal. When we view the things of the world through our prajna-eye, we no longer cling to them; through not clinging to them we become independent of them and finally cease to rely on them as a source of happiness. This is the process of purification suggested by the *Diamond Sutra*.

It is no accident that the *Diamond Sutra* became a core text of the Zen tradition. Not concerned so much with the highly intellectualized and subtle deconstruction of conceptual categories elsewhere in the sutra, the Zen tradition found inspiration in the last stanza, less as a doctrinal summary than as a return to the phenomenal world to see its ephemeral nature.

For early Zen practitioners, each blade of grass, each mountain and river, each passing cloud was as an utterance of the Buddha's teaching. Every aspect of the world of nature became an occasion for Zen followers to celebrate the Buddha's insights. It gave rise to numerous metaphors in Zen poetry and visual arts. The enlightenment poem of Su Tung-po, one of the greatest poets of China, gives flesh and bones to the insights of the *Diamond Sutra*:

> The roaring waterfall is the Buddha's golden mouth.
> The mountains in the distance are his pure luminous body.
> How many thousands of poems have flowed through me
>   tonight!
> And tomorrow I won't be able to repeat even one word.[78]

At the same time, the death poems of the Zen masters of China and Japan are a poignant reminder of the effervescence of life. On his deathbed, the thirteenth-century Japanese Zen master Muju (1226–1312) wrote:

> For eighty-seven years
> A bubble on the sea,
> Windless, waveless,
> Waveless, windless still.[79]

When the Buddha had finished…: The last lines of this section and of the sutra follow the typical pattern of formal endings of the Mahayana sutras, continuing a tradition shared with Pali and non-Buddhist religious texts from ancient India.

Finally, any seeker, whether a Buddhist practitioner or not, could ask: what is unique about these teachings and how are they relevant to our contemporary framework of understanding? A genuine response to this question would be that Buddha's teachings have always been about human suffering and liberation from that suffering. Each human being, at some point in his or her life, must somehow come face to face with an existential despair. The Buddha's antidote to despair was not a metaphysically speculative point of view but an existentially verifiable investigation: the existential despair can be cured only through a wise or transformed view of the human condition—not an intellectualized abstraction, but something integral to one's own life, a view that might enable one to live in the world without clinging or aversion. All subsequent developments in Buddhist tradition are in the service of this view.

The world-view of the *Diamond Sutra* is embedded in the truth of impermanence as an experiential, universal characteristic rather than as a localized event. Its purpose has been to show that all phenomenal appearances are not ultimate reality but constructions or projections of one's own mind, and other passing causal factors. Practitioners should regard all phenomena in this way, as empty of self-nature and inherently tranquil.

My attempt has been to show that it is possible to comprehend the insights of the *Diamond Sutra* through contemporary modes of understanding, such as quantum reality. I have tried to place equal emphasis on the fact that, in order to bear fruit, these insights must transcend intellectual thought and enter the domain of meditation practice. History shows that results are more easily accessible to someone who has had an authentic spiritual or religious experience and sees these teachings as avenues for deepening personal insights.

I have found it useful to refer to the historical context of the composition of the text to show that every generation of Buddhist practitioners has tried to rediscover these insights in unique ways. The *Diamond Sutra* has been revisited and reinvestigated for centuries. As Buddhist teachings become widely disseminated in the West, one hopes that we too shall make a concerted effort to recover these ancient insights in our own way.

Appendix

The Diamond Sutra

THUS HAVE I HEARD. At one time the Buddha was staying at Anatha-pindika's garden in Jeta Grove in the city of Shravasti. With him was a large gathering of 1,250 monks and bodhisattva-mahasattvas. Early in the morning, when the meal time came, the Buddha put on his robe and, holding his bowl, entered the great city of Shravasti where he begged for food. Having finished begging from door to door, he came back to his own seat in the garden and took his meal. When this was done, he put away his robe and bowl, washed his feet, spread his seat, and sat down, mindfully fixing his attention in front of him.

Then the Venerable Subhuti, who was among the assembly, rose from his seat, bared his right shoulder, set his right knee on the ground, and, respectfully folding his hands, addressed the Buddha thus: "It is wonderful, World-Honored One, that the Tathagata thinks so much of all the bodhisattvas and instructs them so well. World-Honored One, in the case of a son or daughter of a good family, who arouses the thought for the supreme awakening, how should they abide in it and how should they keep their thoughts under control?"

The Buddha replied, "Well said, indeed, O Subhuti! As you say, the Tathagata thinks very much of all the bodhisattvas and instructs them well. But now listen attentively and I will tell you how those who have set out on the bodhisattva path should abide in it, and how they should keep their thoughts under control."

"So be it, World-Honored One. I wish to listen to you."

The Buddha said to Subhuti, "All the bodhisattva-mahasattvas, who undertake the practice of meditation, should cherish one thought only: 'When I attain perfect wisdom, I will liberate all sentient beings in every realm of the universe, whether they be egg-born, womb-born, moisture-born, or miraculously born; those with form, those without form, those with perception, those without perception, and those with neither perception nor non-perception. So long as any form of being is conceived, I must allow it to pass into the eternal peace of nirvana, into that realm of nirvana that leaves nothing behind, and to attain final awakening.'

"And yet although immeasurable, innumerable, and unlimited beings have been liberated, truly no being has been liberated. Why? Because no bodhisattva who is a true bodhisattva entertains such concepts as a self, a person, a being, or a living soul. Thus there are no sentient beings to be liberated and no self to attain perfect wisdom.

"Furthermore, Subhuti, in the practice of generosity a bodhisattva should be unsupported. He or she should practice generosity without regard to sight, sound, touch, flavor, smell, or any thought that arises in it. Subhuti, thus should a bodhisattva practice generosity without being supported by any notion of a sign. Why? When a bodhisattva practices generosity without being supported by any notion of a sign, his or her merit will be beyond conception. Subhuti, what do you think? Can you measure the space extending eastward?"

"No, World-Honored One, I cannot."

"Subhuti, can you measure the space extending toward the south, or west, or north, or above, or below?"

"No, World-Honored One, I cannot."

"Subhuti, so it is with the merit of a bodhisattva who practices generosity without cherishing any notion of a sign; it is beyond measure like space. Subhuti, a bodhisattva should persevere one-pointedly in this instruction.

"Subhuti, what do you think? Is it possible to recognize the Tathagata by means of bodily marks?"

"No, World-Honored One. And why? When the Tathagata speaks of the bodily marks, he speaks of the no-possession of no marks."

The Buddha said to Subhuti, "All that has a form is an illusory existence. When the illusory nature of form is perceived, the Tathagata is recognized."

Subhuti said to the Buddha, "World-Honored One, in times to come, will there be beings who, when they hear these teachings, have real faith and confidence in them?"

The Buddha said, "Subhuti, do not utter such words. Five hundred years after the passing of the Tathagata, there will be beings who, having practiced rules of morality and being thus possessed of merit, happen to hear of these statements and will understand their truth. Such beings, you should know, have planted their root of merit not only under one, two, three, four, or five Buddhas, but under countless Buddhas. When such beings, upon hearing these statements, arouse even one moment of pure and clear confidence, the Tathagata will see them and recognize their immeasurable amount of merit. Why? Because all these beings are free from the idea of a self, a person, a being, or a living soul; they are free from the idea of a dharma as well as a no-dharma. Why? Because if they cherish the idea of a dharma, they are still attached to a self, a person, a being, or a living soul. If they cherish the idea of a no-dharma, they are attached to a self, a person, a being, or a living soul. Therefore, do not cherish the idea of a dharma nor that of a no-dharma. For this reason, the Tathagata always preaches thus: 'O you bhikshus, know that my teaching is to be likened unto a raft. Even a dharma is cast aside, much more a no-dharma.'

"Subhuti, what do you think? Has the Tathagata attained the supreme awakening? Has he something he can preach?"

Subhuti said, "World-Honored One, as I understand the teaching of the Buddha, the Buddha has no doctrine to convey. The truth is ungraspable and inexpressible. It neither is nor is not. How is it so? Because all noble teachers are exalted by the unconditioned."

"Subhuti, what do you think? If a son or daughter of a good family should fill the three thousand chiliocosms with the seven precious treasures and give them all as a gift to the Tathagatas, would not the merit thus obtained be great?"

Subhuti said, "Very great, indeed, World-Honored One. Why? Because their merit is characterized with the quality of not being merit. Therefore, the Tathagata speaks of the merit as being great."

The Buddha: "If there is a person who, memorizing even four lines from this sutra, preaches it to others, his merit will be superior to the one just mentioned. Why? Because, Subhuti, all the Buddhas and their supreme awakening issue from this sutra. Subhuti, what is known as the teaching of the Buddha is not the teaching of the Buddha.

"Subhuti, what do you think? Does a srotapanna think, 'I have obtained the fruit of srotapatti'?"

Subhuti said, "No, World-Honored One, he does not. Why? Because while srotapanna means 'entering the stream,' there is no entering here. A true srotapanna is one who does not enter sound, odor, flavor, touch, or any thought that arises."

"Subhuti, what do you think? Does a sakridagamin think, 'I have obtained the fruit of a sakridagamin'?"

Subhuti said, "No, World-Honored One, he does not. Why? Because while sakridagamin means 'going and coming for once,' one who understands that there is really no going-and-coming, he or she is a true sakridagamin."

"Subhuti, what do you think? Does an anagamin think, 'I have obtained the fruit of an anagamin'?"

Subhuti said, "No, World-Honored One, he does not. Why? Because while anagamin means 'not coming,' there is really no not-coming; therefore the one who realizes this is called an anagamin."

"Subhuti, what do you think? Does an arhat think, 'I have obtained arhatship'?"

Subhuti said, "No, World-Honored One, he does not. Why? Because there is no dharma to be called arhat. If, World-Honored One, an arhat thinks, 'I have obtained arhatship,' this means that he has the idea of an ego-self, a person, a living being, or a soul.

"Although the Buddha has said that I am the foremost of those who have obtained aranasamadhi, that I am the foremost of those arhats who are liberated from unwholesome desires, World-Honored One, I cherish no thought that I have attained arhatship. World-Honored One, [if I did] you would not have declared of me, 'Subhuti, who is the foremost of those who dwell in peaceful abiding, does not dwell anywhere; that is why he is called a "dweller in peace."'

The Buddha asked Subhuti, "What do you think? When the Tathagata practiced in ancient times under Dipankara Buddha, did he attain any Dharma?"

"No, World-Honored One, he did not attain any Dharma while practicing with the Dipankara Buddha."

"Subhuti, what do you think? Does a bodhisattva create any harmonious buddha fields?"

"No, World-Honored One, he does not. Why? Because to create a harmonious buddha field is not to create a harmonious buddha field, and therefore it is known as creating a harmonious buddha field."

"So, Subhuti, all bodhisattvas should develop a pure, lucid mind that doesn't depend upon sight, sound, touch, flavor, smell, or any thought that arises in it. A bodhisattva should develop a mind that functions freely, without depending on anything whatsoever."

The Buddha continued, "Subhuti, what do you think? If someone were to have a body as large as Mount Sumeru, would not this body be very large?"

Subhuti said, "Very large indeed, World-Honored One. Why? Because the Buddha teaches that that which is no-body is known as a large body."

"Subhuti, what do you think? If there were as many Ganges Rivers as there are grains of sand in the Ganges, would the number of grains of sand in all those rivers would be many?"

Subhuti said, "Very many, indeed, World-Honored One. Those Ganges Rivers would indeed be many, much more so the grains of sand in them."

"Subhuti, what do you think? If there were a good man or woman who filled the three thousand chiliocosms containing as many world systems as there are grains of sand in those Ganges Rivers with the seven precious treasures and then gave them all away out of generosity, would not this merit be very great?"

Subhuti said, "Very great, indeed, World-Honored One."

The Buddha said, "I declare to you, Subhuti, if a good man or woman were to accept, practice, and explain even four lines of this sutra to others, such merit would be far greater than the preceding one.

"Moreover, Subhuti, wherever this sutra or even four lines of it are preached, that place will be respected by all beings including devas, ashuras, etc., as if it were the Buddha's own shrine or chaitya. How much more [worthy of respect] the person who can memorize and recite this sutra [for the benefit of others]! Subhuti, you should know that such a person achieves the highest, foremost, and most wonderful blessing. Wherever this sutra is kept, the place is to be regarded as if the Buddha or a venerable disciple of his were present."

At that time Subhuti said to the Buddha, "World-Honored One, what will this sutra be called? How should we keep its teachings in mind?"

The Buddha said to Subhuti, "This sutra will be called the *Vajrachedika Prajnaparamita, The Diamond-Cutter Wisdom That Has Gone Beyond,* because it has the capacity to cut through illusions and afflictions and bring us to the shore of awakening, and by this title you will know it.

"And why? The reason is, Subhuti, that what the Tathagata has called the Prajnaparamita, the highest, transcendental wisdom, is not, in fact, the Prajnaparamita and therefore it is called Prajnaparamita.

"Subhuti, what do you think? Is there any Dharma that the Tathagata has taught?"

"No, indeed, World-Honored One, there is none."

"What do you think, Subhuti? Are there many dust particles in the three thousand chiliocosms?"

"Yes, very many, indeed, World-Honored One."

"Subhuti, the Tathagata teaches that what are called dust particles are not dust particles. That is why they are merely dust particles. And what the Tathagata calls chiliocosms are not chiliocosms. That is why they are merely chiliocosms.

"What do you think, Subhuti? Can the Tathagata be recognized through the thirty-two marks [of a great man]?"

"No, World-Honored One, he cannot be recognized through the thirty-two marks. And why? Because the Tathagata has taught that what are called the thirty-two marks are really no-marks. Therefore they are called the thirty-two marks."

"Subhuti, suppose a man or a woman were to renounce all his or her belongings as many times as there are grains of sands in the river Ganges, the merit thus gained would not exceed that of one who, memorizing even one gatha of four lines of this sutra, preaches them to others."

Venerable Subhuti, listening to this discourse, through the shock of the Doctrine, had a deep understanding of the meaning of the sutra and was moved to tears. He said to the Buddha, "It is wonderful, indeed, World-Honored One, how well the Tathagata has taught this discourse on Dharma. Through it [a new level of] cognition has been produced in me. Never before have I heard such a discourse on Dharma. World-Honored One, if someone hears this sutra and has pure and clear confidence in it, that person will gain true perception. And what is called true perception is indeed no-perception. This is what the Tathagata teaches as true perception.

"World-Honored One, it is not difficult for me to have faith in, to understand, and to memorize this sutra, which I have just heard. But in the ages to come, in the next five hundred years, if there are beings who, listening to this sutra, are able to believe, understand, and memorize it, they will indeed be most wonderful beings. In them no perception of a self, a person, a being, or a living soul will take place. And why? Because that which is perception of self is no-perception. That which is perception of a being, a person, or a living soul is no-perception. And why? Because the Buddhas have left all perceptions behind."

The Buddha said to Subhuti, "It is just as you say. If there is a person who, listening to this sutra, is not frightened, alarmed, or disturbed, you should know him as a wonderful person. Why? Because what the Tathagata has taught as *paramaparamita,* the highest perfection, is not the highest perfection and is therefore called the highest perfection.

"Moreover, Subhuti, the teaching of the Tathagata on the perfection of patience is really no perfection and therefore it is the perfection of patience. Why? Subhuti, when, in ancient times, my body was cut to pieces by the king of Kalinga, I did not have the idea of a self, a person, a being, or a living soul. Why? When at that time my body was dismembered limb after limb, joint after joint, feelings of anger and ill will would have arisen in me had I had the idea of a self, a person, a being, or a living soul.

"With my superknowledge I recall that in my past five hundred lifetimes I have led the life of a sage devoted to patience and during those times I did not have the idea of an ego, a person, a being, or a soul.

"Therefore, Subhuti, a bodhisattva, detaching him- or herself from all ideas, should rouse the desire for utmost, supreme, and perfect awakening. He or she should produce thoughts that are unsupported by forms, sounds, smells, tastes, tangible objects, or mind objects, unsupported by Dharma, unsupported by no-Dharma, unsupported by everything. And why? Because all supports are no supports. This is the reason why the Buddha teaches that a bodhisattva should practice generosity without dwelling on form. Subhuti, the reason he practices generosity is to benefit all beings.

"The Tathagata teaches that all ideas are no-ideas and that all beings are no-beings. Subhuti, the Tathagata is one who speaks of things as they are, speaks what is true, and speaks in accordance with reality. He does not speak deceptively or to please people. Subhuti, in the Dharma attained by the Tathagata there is neither truth nor falsehood.

"Subhuti, if a bodhisattva should practice generosity while still depending on form, he or she is like someone walking in the dark. He or she will not see anything. But when a bodhisattva practices generosity without depending on form, he or she is like someone with good eyesight walking in the bright sunshine—he or she can see all shapes and colors.

"Subhuti, if in times to come the sons and daughters of good families memorize and recite this sutra, they will be seen and recognized by the Tathagata with his buddha knowledge, and they will all acquire immeasurable and infinite merit.

"Furthermore, Subhuti, if one should renounce in the morning all one's belongings as many times as there are grains of sand in the River Ganges, and if one should do likewise at noon and in the evening and continue thus for countless ages; and if someone else, on hearing this discourse on Dharma, were to accept it with a believing heart, the merit acquired by the latter would far exceed that of the former. How much more the merit of one who would copy, memorize, learn, recite, and expound it for others!

"Subhuti, to sum up, immeasurable, innumerable, and incomprehensible is this discourse on Dharma. The Tathagata has taught it for the well-being of those who have set out in the best, in the most excellent vehicle.

Those who take up this discourse on Dharma, bear it in mind, recite, study, and expound it in detail for others will all be known to the Tathagata and recognized by him and acquire merit that is incomparable, measureless, and infinite. Such beings will share in the supreme awakening attained by the Tathagata. Why? Because, Subhuti, this course on the Dharma could not be understood by beings of inferior resolve, nor by those attached to the idea of a self, a person, a being, or a living soul. [Being so caught up], they are unable to hear, memorize, learn, recite, and expound this sutra.

"Moreover, Subhuti, the spot of earth where this sutra will be revealed, that spot of earth will be worthy of worship by the whole world with its gods, men, ashuras, worthy of being saluted respectfully, worthy of being honored by circumambulation. That spot of earth will be like a shrine or temple.

"And yet Subhuti, there will be some sons and daughters of good families who will be despised for their memorizing and reciting of this sutra. This is due to their previous evil karma. The impure deeds that these beings have done in their former lives are liable to lead them into states of woe in this lifetime. But [if they are not averse to] being despised in the present life, whatever evil karma they produced in their previous lives will be destroyed, and they will be able to attain the awakening of a Buddha.

"Subhuti, with my superknowledge, I recall that in the past, even before I was with Dipankara Buddha, I made offerings, and had been attendant, to eighty-four thousand multi-million Buddhas. But the merit I gained from that service is not one hundredth nor even one hundredth million of the merit of someone who, at the time of the collapse of the Dharma, memorizes, recites, and learns from this sutra and expound it to others. It bears neither number, nor fraction, nor enumeration, nor similarity, nor comparison, nor resemblance.

"Moreover, Subhuti, the merit acquired by good men and women who, at the time of the collapse of the Dharma, memorize, recite, and learn this sutra will be so great that if I were to describe it in detail, some people would become suspicious and disbelieving, and their minds might become disoriented. Subhuti, you should know that the meaning of this sutra is beyond comprehension and discussion. Likewise, the fruit that results from receiving and practicing this sutra is beyond comprehension and discussion."

At that time, the Venerable Subhuti said to the Buddha, "World-

Honored One, may I ask you again? If the sons and daughters of good family wish to arouse the thought of supreme enlightenment, how should they abide in it? How should they keep their thought under control?"

The Buddha replied, "Someone who has set out on the bodhisattva path should cherish one thought only: 'When I attain perfect wisdom, I will liberate all sentient beings in every realm of the universe, whether they be egg-born, womb-born, moisture-born, miraculously born; those with form, those without form, those with perception, those without perception, and those with neither perception nor non-perception so long as any form of being is conceived, I must allow it to pass into the eternal peace of nirvana, into that realm of nirvana that leaves nothing behind, and to attain final awakening.'

"And yet, although immeasurable, innumerable, and unlimited beings have been liberated, truly no being has been liberated. Why, Subhuti? Because if a bodhisattva entertains such thoughts as a self, a person, a being, or a living soul, he is not a true bodhisattva.

"Subhuti, in fact, there is no independently existing object of mind called the supreme, perfect awakening. What do you think, Subhuti? In ancient times, when the Tathagata was living with Dipankara Buddha, did he attain anything called the supreme, perfect awakening?"

"No, World-Honored One. According to what I understand, there is no attainment of anything called the supreme, perfect awakening."

The Buddha said, "Right you are! It is for this reason that the Dipankara Buddha then predicted of me: 'You, young Brahmin, will be in a future time a Tathagata, an arhat, fully enlightened, by the name of Shakyamuni!' This prediction was made because there is, in fact, nothing that can be attained that is called the supreme, perfect awakening.

"Why is this? Because, Subhuti, 'Tathagata' is synonymous with true suchness (tathata) of all dharmas. And if someone were to say, 'The Tathagata has fully known the utmost, right, and perfect liberation,' he would be speaking falsely. Why? Because there is no Dharma by which the Tathagata has fully known the utmost, right, and perfect awakening. And the Dharma that the Tathagata has fully known and demonstrated is neither graspable nor elusive. Therefore the Tathagata teaches 'All dharmas are the Buddha's own and special Dharmas.' Why? All dharmas, Subhuti, have been taught by the Tathagata as no-dharmas. Therefore all dharmas are expediently called the Buddha's own and special Dharmas.

"Subhuti, a comparison can be made with the idea of a great human body. What the Tathagata calls a great body is in fact a no-body. So it is, Subhuti, with the bodhisattvas. If a bodhisattva were to think, 'I will lead all beings to nirvana,' he or she should not be considered a bodhisattva. Why? Because there is no such thing as a 'bodhi being' (bodhi sattva). It is because of this that the Tathagata teaches that all dharmas are without the notion of a self, a person, a being, or a living soul.

"Subhuti, furthermore, if a bodhisattva were to say, 'I will create harmonious buddha fields,' he or she likewise should not be called a bodhi being. Why? The Tathagata has taught that the harmonious buddha fields are not in fact harmonious buddha fields. Such is merely a name. It is thus that he speaks of truly harmonious buddha fields.

"Subhuti, a bodhisattva who thoroughly understands the principle of no-self and no-dharma as the true self and the true Dharma [respectively] is to be considered an authentic bodhisattva.

"Subhuti, what do you think? Does the Tathagata possess the human eye?"
Subhuti replied, "Yes, World-Honored One, he does."

"Subhuti, what do you think? Does the Tathagata possess the divine eye?"
"Yes, World-Honored One, he does."

"Subhuti, what do you think? Does the Tathagata possess the gnostic eye?"
"Yes, World-Honored One, he does."

"Subhuti, what do you think? Does the Tathagata possess the prajna eye?"
"Yes, World-Honored One, he does."

"Subhuti, what do you think? Does the Tathagata possess the buddha eye?"
"Yes, World-Honored One, he does."

"Subhuti, what do you think? Has the Tathagata taught about the grains of sand in the Ganges River?"
"Yes, World-Honored One, he has."

"Subhuti, what do you think? If there were as many Ganges Rivers as there are grains of sand in the Ganges River and if there were a buddha land for each one of those grains of sand, would those buddha lands be many?"
"Yes, World-Honored One, they would be many indeed."

"Subhuti, I declare to you that however many living beings there may be in all of these manifold buddha lands and though each one of them has numerous trends of thought, the Tathagata has known them all. How is it so? Because the Tathagata teaches that all trends of thought are actually not trends of thought, and that is why he calls them trends of thought. Why? Because the past mind cannot be gotten hold of, the future mind cannot be gotten hold of, and the present mind cannot be gotten hold of.

"What do you think, Subhuti? If a son or daughter of good family were to fill the three thousand chiliocosms with the seven precious treasures and then give them as a gift to the Tathagatas, the arhats, the fully enlightened ones, would the merit of that act be great?"

Subhuti replied, "Yes, it would be great indeed, O Lord."

The Buddha said, "So it is, Subhuti, so it is. But if, in reality, there were such a thing as a great heap of merit, the Tathagata would not have spoken of it as a great heap of merit. Such is merely a name. It is because it is without a foundation that the Tathagata has spoken of it as a great heap of merit."

"What do you think, Subhuti? Can the Tathagata be seen by means of his perfectly formed body?"

Subhuti said, "No, World-Honored One. As I understand it, the Tathagata is not to be seen by means of his perfectly formed body. Why? Because the Tathagata has taught that what is called a perfectly formed body is not a perfectly formed body. Such is merely a name. Therefore it is called a perfectly formed body."

The Buddha asked further, "What do you think, Subhuti? Can the Tathagata be seen by means of his possession of bodily marks?"

Subhuti replied, "No, World-Honored One. As I understand it, the Tathagata cannot be by means of his possession of the bodily marks. Why? Because the Tathagata has taught that what are called the bodily marks are not in fact bodily marks. Such is merely a name. Therefore they are called the bodily marks."

The Buddha asked, "What do you think, Subhuti? Does the Tathagata think, 'by me has Dharma been taught'? Subhuti, whosoever says that the Tathagata thinks this way slanders the Tathagata; he would misrepresent me by seizing on what is not there. Why? The Tathagata has taught that in the teaching of the Dharma there is no Dharma that can be pointed to as Dharma. Such is merely a name. That is why it is called the teaching of Dharma."

Subhuti asked, "World-Honored One, will there be beings in the future, five hundred years from now, at the time of the collapse of the Dharma, who will truly believe these teachings?"

The Buddha said, "Subhuti, there are neither beings nor no-beings. Why? The Tathagata has taught that what are called beings are truly no beings. Such is merely a name. That is why the Tathagata has spoken of them as beings.

"Subhuti, what do you think? Is there any Dharma by [means of] which the Tathagata has understood perfect, unexcelled awakening?"

Subhuti said, "No, World-Honored One. As I understand it, there is no Dharma by which the Tathagata has understood perfect, unexcelled awakening."

The Buddha said, "So it is, Subhuti, so it is. Not even the least trace of Dharma is to be found anywhere. Such is merely a name. That is why it is called the perfect, unexcelled awakening.

"Furthermore, Subhuti, the dharma called the anuttara samyaksambodhi is at one with everything else. Nothing in it is at variance with anything else. That is why it is called the perfect, unexcelled awakening. It is self-identical through the absence of a self, a person, a being, or a living soul, and that is why it is fully known as the totality of all the wholesome dharmas. And yet, Subhuti, no dharmas have been taught by the Tathagata. Such is merely a name. Thus are they called 'wholesome dharmas.'"

"Again, Subhuti, if a son or daughter of a good family were to pile up the seven precious treasures in the three thousand chiliocosms and give them away as a gift, the merit resulting from such an act would be much less than that of someone who was to memorize but one stanza from this *Vajrachedika Prajnaparamita* and teach it to others. The merit of the latter would indeed be so great that no comparison could be made.

"Subhuti, you must not think that the Tathagata entertains the notion 'I will bring all living beings to the shore of awakening.' Why? Because in reality there are no beings who can be liberated by the Tathagata. To entertain the notion that there are beings who can be liberated would be to partake in the idea of a self, a person, a being and a living soul. The Tathagata has taught that one must not seize upon these notions, and yet foolish common people have seized upon them. Subhuti, though the Tathagata uses the words 'foolish common people,' in reality there are no such people. Such is merely a name. That is why they are called foolish common people.

"Subhuti, what do you think? Is the Tathagata to be recognized by means of his possession of [bodily] marks?"

Subhuti replied, "No, World-Honored One."

The Buddha said, "If, Subhuti, the Tathagata could be recognized by means of his possession of [bodily] marks, then the *chakravartin* also would be a Tathagata. Therefore the Tathagata is not to be recognized by means of his possession of [bodily] marks."

Subhuti said, "As I understand the Tathagata's teaching, he is not to be recognized by means of his [bodily] marks."

Then the Buddha uttered the following stanzas:

Those who saw me through my form,
And those who heard me by my voice,
False endeavors they engaged in;
Me those people will not see.

A Buddha is to be seen [known] through the Dharma,
And his guidance manifests from Dharma bodies.
Yet the true nature of the Dharma cannot be understood,
And no one can be conscious of it as an object.

"Subhuti, you should not think that the Tathagata has attained the anuttara samyaksambodhi by virtue of his possession of the thirty-two [bodily] marks. Why? Because the Tathagata could not have attained the anuttara samyaksambodhi through possession of [bodily] marks [alone].

"At the same time, Subhuti, no one should say that those who have set out on the path of the bodhisattva need to see all dharmas in terms of their annihilation. I declare to you, Subhuti, that those who set out in the bodhisattvayana do not entertain any notion of the annihilation of dharmas.

"Again, Subhuti, if a son or daughter of good family were to fill as many world systems as there are grains of sands in the Ganges River with the seven precious treasures and give them as a gift to the Tathagatas, arhats, fully enlightened ones, and if, on the other hand, a bodhisattva were to gain the insight that all dharmas are empty and have no self-nature or essence of their own, his or her merit would be immeasurably and incalculably [greater than that of the former]. Why is that? Because bodhisattvas are immune to any rewards of merit."

Subhuti asked, "What does it mean, World-Honored One, that the bodhisattvas are immune to rewards of merit?"

The Buddha said, "The bodhisattva whose merit is great does not get caught in the desire for or idea of merit. She or he understands that such is merely a name. It is for this reason that the bodhisattva is immune to the rewards of merit.

"Whosoever says that the Tathagata goes or comes, stands, sits or lies down does not understand the meaning of my teaching. Why? The Tathagata does not come from anywhere, nor does he depart to anywhere. Therefore he is called the Tathagata, the arhat, the fully enlightened one.

"Subhuti, what do you think? If a son or daughter of good family were to grind as many world systems as there are particles of dust in the three thousand chiliocosms as finely as they can be ground with incalculable vigor, would that be an enormous collection of dust particles?"

Subhuti replied, "Yes, World-Honored One, it would indeed be an enormous collection. Why? If the dust particles had any real self-existence, the Tathagata would not have called them an enormous collection of dust particles. As I understand it, what the Tathagata calls a collection of dust particles is not in essence a collection of dust particles. Such is merely a name. It is for this reason that it is called a collection of dust particles. Moreover, what the Tathagata has taught as the system of three thousand chiliocosms is not in fact a system of chiliocosms. That is why they are called chiliocosms. To consider the chiliocosms as real would be a case of seizing on a material object that is nothing but an assembly of dust particles. That is why it is called seizing on an object."

The Buddha added, "What is called seizing upon a material object is a matter of linguistic convention without factual content. It is not a dharma or a no-dharma. And yet the foolish common people have seized upon it.

"Subhuti, what do you think? If someone were to say that the Tathagata has taught the view of self, person, being, or living soul, would that person have understood my meaning?"

Subhuti replied, "No, World-Honored One, such a person would not have understood the Tathagata. Why? What the Tathagata calls a self-view, a person-view, a being-view, or a living soul-view are not in essence a self-view, a person-view, a being-view, or a living soul-view. That is why they are called a self-view, a person-view, a being-view, or a living soul-view."

The Buddha said, "It is in this manner, Subhuti, that someone who has set out on the bodhisattva path should know all dharmas, see that all dharmas are like this, and should have confidence in the understanding of all dharmas without any conception of dharmas. Subhuti, what the Tathagata has called a conception of dharmas is not a conception of dharmas. Such is merely a name. That is why it is called a conception of dharmas.

"Again, Subhuti, if a son or daughter of good family were to pile up the seven precious treasures in all the three thousand chiliocosms and give them away as a gift to the Tathagatas, the arhats, and the fully enlightened ones, and, on the other hand, if someone were to take but one stanza from this *Vajrachedika Prajnaparamita* and bear it in mind, teach it, recite and study it, and illuminate it in full detail for others, his or her merit would be much more immeasurable and incalculable [than that of the former]. And in what spirit would he or she illuminate it for others? Without being caught up in the appearances of things in themselves but understanding the nature of things just as they are. Why? Because:

So you should view all of the fleeting worlds:
A star at dawn, a bubble in the stream;
A flash of lightning in a summer cloud;
A flickering lamp, a phantom, and a dream.

When the Buddha had finished [speaking], Venerable Subhuti, the monks and nuns, the pious lay men and women, the bodhisattvas, and the whole world with its gods, ashuras, and *gandharvas* were filled with joy at the teaching, and, taking it to heart, they went their separate ways.

Notes

1. Mu Soeng, *Heart Sutra: Ancient Buddhism Wisdom in the Light of Quantum Reality* (Cumberland, RI: Primary Point Press, 1991).

2. This term is used here in the generic Indian religious sense indicating a great yogic adept and not in the sense of the later Tantric tradition.

3. Edward Conze, *Buddhism: Its Essence and Development* (New York: Harper and Row, 1951, 1959), pp. 81–85, 103–5, 174–76.

4. A.L. Basham, *The Wonder That Was India* (New York: Grove Press, 1954), pp. 243–47.

5. Michael Carrithers, *The Buddha* (Oxford: Oxford University Press, 1983), p. 11.

6. Holger Kalweit, *Dreamtime and Innerspace* (Boston: Shambhala Publications, 1988), p. xii.

7. Carrithers, pp. 21–22.

8. Trevor Ling, *The Buddha* (London: Temple Smith, 1973) p. 106.

9. Sukumar Dutt, *The Buddha and Five After-Centuries* (Calcutta: Sahitya Samsad, 1978), p. 123.

10. *Kalama Sutta,* Anguttara Nikaya, III. 65. (See p. 95.)

11. Donald Lopez, Jr., ed., *Buddhism in Practice* (Princeton: Princeton University Press, 1995), p. 7.

12. Ibid., p. 5.

13. Edward Conze, *A Short History of Buddhism* (London: Unwin Paperbacks, 1969, 1988), p. 35.

14. Ibid., p. 16.

15. Jonathan S. Walters, "Gotami's Story" in *Buddhism in Practice,* ed. Lopez, p. 114.

16. Conze, *Short History,* p. 45.

17. Heinrich Dumoulin, *Zen Buddhism: A History,* vol. 1 (New York: Macmillan, 1988), p. 35.

18. Hajime Nakamura, "Mahayana Buddhism" in *Buddhism and Asian History,* ed. Joseph Kitagawa and Mark Cummings (New York: Macmillan, 1989), p. 216.

19. Paul Williams, *Mahayana Buddhism* (London: Routledge, 1989), pp. 37, 39.

20. Lama Anagarika Govinda, *Way of the Clouds* (Boulder: Shambhala, 1970), p. 151.

21. Williams, p. 23.

22. Ibid., p. 24.

23. Ibid., p. 26.

24. Ibid., pp. 27–28.

25. Robert Thurman in Lex Hixon, *Mother of the Buddhas: Meditation on the Prajnaparamita Sutra* (Wheaton, IL.: Quest Books, 1993), p. xiii.

26. F. L. Woodward, trans., *The Book of the Kindred Sayings: Samyutta Nikaya,* vol. 5.

27. Bhikkhu Bodhi, trans., *Majjhima Nikaya: The Middle Length Sayings of the Buddha* (Boston: Wisdom Publications, 1995), pp. 229 (*Alagaddupama Sutta,* 22: 13–14.)

28. Precept document calligraphy by Zen Master Seung Sahn, archives of Kwan Um Zen School, Providence, R.I.

29. H. Saddhatissa, trans., *The Sutta Nipata, Navasutta* (London: Curzon Press, 1985), pp. 35–36.

30. Kisa Gotami had lost her only child and had gone mad with grief. She carried the corpse of her child to every teacher in the area and asked them if they could revive her dead son, only to be laughed at by all those she went to see for succor. When she came to the Bud-

dha and asked if he could revive her dead son, the Buddha merely said, "Yes, but on one condition." Kisa was more than willing to fulfill any condition and asked the Buddha what was required. The Buddha asked her to go to the nearby village and knock on each door and find a family in which no one had ever died. From such a family, she was to collect a few grains of mustard seeds and bring these seeds back to the Buddha. With great hope and expectation, Kisa went from door to door, only to be told that someone—a grandparent, a sibling, a spouse, a child—had indeed died in that house. At the end of her round, Kisa herself came to a realization that death visits each and every one without discrimination. Chastened and sober now, she came back to the Buddha, shared her insight and allowed the body of her dead child to be cremated. She became an ordained disciple of the Buddha and was proclaimed an arhat.

31. Conze, *Short History*, p. 50.

32. Richard Robinson and Willard Johnson, *The Buddhist Religion: A Historical Introduction* (Fourth edition; Belmont, CA: Wadsworth Publishing, 1997), p. 86.

33. Ibid., p. 86.

34. Ibid., p. 87.

35. George Leonard, *The Silent Pulse* (New York: E.P. Dutton, 1978), quoted in Mu Soeng, *Heart Sutra*, pp. 18–19.

36. Jack Kornfield, "The Smile of the Buddha: Paradigms in Perspective" in *Ancient Wisdom and Modern Science*, ed. Stanislav Graf (Albany: State University of New York Press, 1984), quoted in Mu Soeng, *Heart Sutra*, pp. 19–20.

37. Mu Soeng, *Heart Sutra*, pp. 17–21.

38. Michael Talbot, *The Holographic Universe* (New York: Harper Perennial, 1992), p. 47.

39. Ibid., pp. 47–48.

40. Hajime Nakamura, "The Career of the Bodhisattva," in *Buddhism and Asian History*, ed. Kitagawa and Cummings, p. 367.

41. Charles Prebish, *Historical Dictionary of Buddhism* (Metuchen, NJ: Scarecrow Press, 1993), p. 75.

42. Hajime Nakamura, *Indian Buddhism: A Survey with Bibliographic Notes* (Delhi: Motilal Banarsidass, 1980), p. 160.

43. Recent scholarship, however, has questioned the historicity of Hui-neng and the concomitant biographical details that have come down to us through the "autobiographical" *Platform Sutra*. See John McRae, *The Northern School and the Formation of Early Ch'an Buddhism* (Honolulu: University of Hawaii Press, 1986) for a comprehensive discussion of this development.

44. Robinson and Johnson, p. 84.

45. Gerald Doherty, "Form is Emptiness: Reading the Diamond Sutra," *The Eastern Buddhist* 16, no. 2 (1983).

46. David Lodge, quoted in Stephen Batchelor, *Awakening of the West* (Berkeley: Parallax Press, 1996), p. 273.

47. Thich Nhat Hanh, *Diamond That Cuts through Illusion* (Berkeley: Parallax Press, 1992), p. 29.

48. *Suttanipata*, 845. Another possible rendering is as follows: "A great man conducting himself in the world free from those [views]/ would not dispute or grasp them."

49. Edward Conze, *Buddhist Wisdom Books: Diamond Sutra and Heart Sutra* (New York: Harper and Row, 1958), p. 45.

50. Reginald Ray, *Buddhist Saints in India: A Study in Buddhist Values and Orientation* (New York: Oxford University Press, 1994), pp. 52–53.

51. For a discussion of this term, see pp. 89–90.

52. Bhikkhu Bodhi, *A Comprehensive Manual of Abhidhamma* (Kandy, Sri Lanka: Buddhist Publication Society, 1993), p. 188.

53. Lex Hixon, *The Mother of the Buddhas*, p. 5.

54. Ibid., p. 9.

55. Ibid., p. 10.

56. Conze, *Buddhist Wisdom Books*, p. 26.

57. Conze, *Vajracchedika Prajnaparamita* in *Minor Buddhist Texts*, ed. Giuseppe Tucci (Delhi: Motilal Banarsidass, 1956, 1986), pp. 95–96.

58. I.B. Horner, *The Book of Discipline* (London: Pali Text Society, 1975), vol. 5, x.1.6.

59. John Blofeld, trans., *The Zen Teaching of Huang Po* (New York: Grove Press, 1958), pp. 64–65.

60. F. L. Woodward, *The Book of Kindred Sayings,* vol. 5, pp. 173–75.

61. Sangharakshita, *Wisdom Beyond Words: Sense and Non-Sense in the Buddhist Prajnaparamita Tradition* (Glasgow: Windhorse Publications, 1993), p. 41.

62. *Abhidharmakosa* iii. 73–74; *Manorathapurani* ii. 340–41.

63. *The New York Times,* September 8, 1996.

64. I.B. Horner, *Minor Anthologies of the Pali Canon, Part IV, Vimanavatthu: Stories of the Mansions,* p. xvi.

65. Frank Reynolds and Charles Hallisey, "The Buddha" in *Buddhism and Asian History,* ed. Kitagawa and Cummings, p. 33.

66. Luis O. Gomez, "Buddhism in India" in *Buddhism and Asian History,* ed. Kitagawa and Cummings, p. 80.

67. Bhikku Bodhi, trans., *Sankharupapatti Sutta* (Majjhima Nikaya, 120), among other references.

68. Joanna Macy, *Mutual Causality in Buddhism and General Systems Theory: The Dharma of Natural Systems* (Albany: State University of New York Press, 1991), p. 92.

69. Ibid., p. 86.

70. Garma C.C. Chang, *The Buddhist Teaching of Totality* (University Park, PA: Pennsylvania State University, 1977), pp. 165–66.

71. Bhikkhu Bodhi, p. 146.

72. Lopez, *Buddhism in Practice,* p. 5.

73. Conze, *Buddhist Wisdom Books,* p. 52.

74. Charles Luk, *Ch'an and Zen Teaching* (Berkeley: Shambhala, 1970), vol. 1, p. 149.

75. Gregory Schopen, "The Manuscript of the Vajracchedika Found at Gilgit" in *Studies in the Literature of The Great Vehicle,* ed. Luis O.

Gomez and Jonathan A. Silk (Ann Arbor: University of Michigan, 1989), p. 133.

76. Thomas Cleary, *Shobogenzo: Zen Essays by Dogen* (Honolulu: University of Hawaii Press, 1986), p. 32.

77. Thich Nhat Hanh, p. 92.

78. Quoted in Stephen Mitchell, ed., *Dropping Ashes on the Buddha: The Teaching of Zen Master Seung Sahn* (New York: Grove Press, 1976), p. 132.

79. Quoted in Lucien Styrk and Takashi Ikemoto, *Zen Poems of China and Japan* (New York: Grove Press, 1973), p. 65.

Bibliography

Basham, A.L. *The Wonder That Was India.* New York: Grove Press, 1954.

Batchelor, Stephen. *Awakening of the West.* Berkeley: Parallax Press, 1996.

Blofeld, John, trans. *The Zen Teaching of Huang Po.* New York: Grove Press, 1958.

Bodhi, Bhikku, trans. *Majjhima Nikaya: The Middle Length Sayings of the Buddha.* Boston: Wisdom Publications, 1995.

Bodhi, Bhikkhu, trans. *A Comprehensive Manual of Abhidhamma.* Kandy, Sri Lanka: Buddhist Publication Society, 1993.

Carrithers, Michael. *The Buddha.* Oxford: Oxford University Press, 1983.

Chang, Garma C.C. *The Buddhist Teaching of Totality.* University Park, PA: Pennsylvania State University, 1977.

Cleary, Thomas. *Shobogenzo: Zen Essays by Dogen.* Honolulu: University of Hawaii Press, 1986.

Conze, Edward. *Buddhism: Its Essence and Development.* New York: Harper and Row, 1951, 1959.

———. *Buddhist Wisdom Books: Diamond Sutra and Heart Sutra.* New York: Harper and Row, 1958.

———trans. *The Perfection of Widsom in Eight Thousand Lines and Its Verse Summary.* Bolinas, CA: Four Seasons Foundation, 1973.

———. *A Short History of Buddhism.* London: Unwin Paperbacks, 1969, 1988.

———. *Short Prajnaparamita Texts.* London: Luzac and Co., 1974.

Dumoulin, Heinrich. *Zen Buddhism: A History.* Vol. 1. NewYork: Macmillan, 1988.

Dutt, Sukumar. *The Buddha and Five After-Centuries.* Calcutta: Sahitya Samsad, 1978.

Eastern Buddhist. Kyoto: Otani University.

Gomez, Louis O., and Jonathan A. Silk, eds. *Studies in the Literature of The Great Vehicle.* Ann Arbor: University of Michigan, 1989.

Govinda, Lama Anagarika. *Way of the Clouds.* Boulder: Shambhala, 1970.

Hixon, Lex. *The Mother of the Buddhas: Meditation on the Prajnaparamita Sutra.* Wheaton, IL.: Quest Books, 1993.

Horner, I.B. *The Book of Discipline.* London: Pali Text Society, 1975.

Kalweit, Holger. *Dreamtime and Innerspace.* Boston: Shambhala Publications, 1988.

Kitagawa, Joseph, and Mark Cummings, eds. *Buddhism and Asian History.* New York: Macmillan, 1989.

Lancaster, Lewis, ed. *Prajnaparamita and Related Systems: Studies in Honor of Edward Conze.* Berkeley: Berkeley Buddhist Studies Series, University of California, 1977.

Ling, Trevor. *The Buddha.* London: Temple Smith, 1973.

Lopez, Donald, Jr., ed. *Buddhism in Practice.* Princeton: Princeton University Press, 1995.

Luk, Charles. *Ch'an and Zen Teaching.* Vol. 1. Berkeley: Shambhala, 1970.

Macy, Joanna. *Mutual Causality in Buddhism and General Systems Theory: The Dharma of Natural Systems.* Albany: State University of New York Press, 1991.

McRae, John. *The Northern School and the Formation of Early Ch'an Buddhism.* Honolulu: University of Hawaii Press, 1986.

Mitchell, Stephen, ed. *Dropping Ashes on the Buddha: The Teaching of Zen Master Seung Sahn.* New York: Grove Press, 1976.

Mu Soeng. *Heart Sutra: Ancient Buddhism Wisdom in the Light of Quantum Reality.* Cumberland, RI: Primary Point Press, 1991.

Murcott, Susan. *The First Buddhist Women.* Berkeley: Parallax Press, 1991.

Nakamura, Hajime. *Indian Buddhism: A Survey with Bibliographical Notes.* Delhi: Motilal Banarsidass, 1980.

Nhat Hanh, Thich. *Diamond That Cuts through Illusion.* Berkeley: Parallax Press, 1992.

Prebish, Charles. *Historical Dictionary of Buddhism.* Metuchen, NJ: Scarecrow Press, 1993.

Price, A. F., and Wong Mu. *The Diamond Sutra and the Sutra of Huineng.* Boston: Shambhala Publications, 1969, 1990.

Robinson, Richard, and Willard Johnson. *The Buddhist Religion: A Historical Introduction.* Fourth edition. Belmont, CA: Wadsworth Publishing, 1997.

Ray, Reginald. *Buddhist Saints in India: A Study in Buddhist Values and Orientation.* New York: Oxford University Press, 1994.

Saddhatissa, H., trans. *The Sutta Nipata.* London: Curzon Press, 1985.

Sangharakshita. *Wisdom Beyond Words: Sense and Non-Sense in the Buddhist Prajnaparamita Tradition.* Glasgow: Windhorse Publications, 1993.

Schober, Julian, ed. *Sacred Biography in the Buddhist Traditions of South and Southeast Asia.* Honolulu: University of Hawaii Press, 1997.

Styrk, Lucien, and Takashi Ikemoto. *Zen Poems of China and Japan.* New York: Grove Press, 1973.

Strong, John, ed. *The Experience of Buddhism: Sources and Interpretations.* Belmont, CA: Wadsworth, 1995.

Talbot, Michael. *The Holographic Universe.* New York: Harper Perennial, 1992.

Tucci, Giuseppe, ed. *Minor Buddhist Texts.* Parts I and II. Delhi: Motilal Banarsidass, 1956, 1986.

Warder, A. K. *Indian Buddhism.* Second revised edition. Delhi: Motilal Banarsidass, 1970.

Williams, Paul. *Mahayana Buddhism.* London: Routledge, 1989.

Woodward, F. L., trans. *Samyutta Nikaya: The Book of the Kindred Sayings.* Vol. 5. Oxford: Pali Text Society, 1930, 1979.

Index

Trust in Mind
The Rebellion of Chinese Zen
Mu Soeng
Foreword by Jan Chozen Bays
224 pages, ISBN 0-86171-391-5, $16.95

The Great Way is not difficult for those who have no preferences. When love and hate are both absent, everything becomes clear and undisguised. Make the smallest distinction, however, and heaven and earth are set infinitely apart.

...So begins "Trust in Mind," the beloved poem that is often considered the first historical document in the Zen tradition. It remains an anchor of Zen Buddhist practice to this day.

Here, scholar and commentator Mu Soeng explores the poem's importance and impact in three sections: The Dharma of Trust in Mind, The Tao of Trust in Mind, and The Chan of Trust in Mind. Finally, a brilliant line-by-line commentary brings the elements of this ancient work completely to life for the modern reader.

Trust in Mind is the first book of its kind to look at this very important Zen text from historical and cultural contexts, as well as from the practitioner's point of view.

"Mu Soeng's elegant commentary seamlessly marries the precision of the scholar with the heart of the practitioner. In his hands, the poem comes alive with meaning, addressing a challenge with which we all wrestle: how to live at ease in this complex and difficult world. This book will be a comfort and a refuge to many; it has already joined other spiritual classics as a permanent resident of my reading table."—Stephen Cope, author of *Yoga and the Quest for the True Self*

"Along with his own astute commentary, Mu Soeng offers us a number of different translations of the poem side by side. Both a mind training and a lesson in Buddhist history, *Trust in Mind* reveals the beauty and profundity of a Dharma masterpiece."—*Inquiring Mind*

WISDOM'S TEACHINGS OF THE BUDDHA SERIES

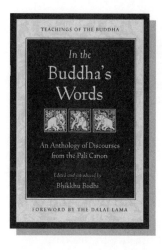

In the Buddha's Words
An Anthology of Discourses
from the Pāli Canon
Edited and introduced by Bhikkhu Bodhi
Foreword by the Dalai Lama
512 pages, ISBN 0-86171-491-1, $18.95

This landmark collection is the definitive introduction to the Buddha's teachings—in his own words. The American scholar-monk Bhikkhu Bodhi, whose voluminous translations have won widespread acclaim, here presents selected discourses of the Buddha from the Pāli Canon, the earliest record of what the Buddha taught. Divided into ten thematic chapters, *In the Buddha's Words* reveals the full scope of the Buddha's discourses, from family life and marriage to renunciation and the path of insight. A concise, informative introduction precedes each chapter, guiding the reader toward a deeper understanding of the texts that follow.

In the Buddha's Words allows even readers unacquainted with Buddhism to grasp the significance of the Buddha's contributions to our world heritage. Taken as a whole, these texts bear eloquent testimony to the breadth and intelligence of the Buddha's teachings, and point the way to an ancient yet ever-vital path. Students and seekers alike will find this systematic presentation indispensable.

The Middle Length Discourses of the Buddha

A Translation of the Majjhima Nikaya
Translated by Bhikkhu Nanamoli and Bhikkhu Bodhi
1424 pages, cloth, ISBN 0-86171-072-X, $65.00

Winner of the *Choice* Outstanding Academic Book Award and the *Tricycle* Prize for Excellence in Buddhist Publishing.

"Brilliant, scholarly, and eminently readable."—Joseph Goldstein, author of *One Dharma*

The Connected Discourses of the Buddha

A Translation of the Samyutta Nikaya
Translated by Bhikkhu Bodhi
2080 pages, cloth, ISBN 0-86171-331-1, $95.00

"Bhikkhu Bodhi has translated the discourses of the Buddha; no one is better qualified. Collected into their different themes, *The Connected Discourses* points the way to enlightenment. This book serves as one of the finest resources available for insight into the human condition. The Buddha addresses issues such as body/mind, daily life realities, suffering and joy, awareness and meditation. This book is rich in spiritual teachings, and is suitable for daily reflection, study, as a manual for psychologists, and as a teaching guide at universities. It offers a wealth of benefits to anyone interested in the true heart of the Buddha's teachings."—Christopher Titmuss, author of *Light on Enlightenment* and *An Awakened Life*

"To hold a copy of *The Connected Discourses of the Buddha* is to hold treasure in your hands. Bhikkkhu Bodhi has, once again, made the ancient words of the Buddha come alive. Timely and significant, highly readable, and invaluable."—*Eastern Horizon*

The Long Discourses of the Buddha
A Translation of the Digha Nikaya
Translated by Maurice Walshe
656 pages, cloth, ISBN 0-86171-103-3, $45.00

"An amazing work that speaks to us across 2,500 years. Each person who undertakes to read and study *The Long Discourses of the Buddha* will open up new paths of thought, and new and precious insights, into the depths of Buddhist history and thought."
—*Mountain Record*

ABOUT WISDOM

Wisdom Publications, a nonprofit publisher, is dedicated to making available authentic Buddhist works for the benefit of all. We publish translations of the sutras and tantras, commentaries and teachings of past and contemporary Buddhist masters, and original works by the world's leading Buddhist scholars. We publish our titles with the appreciation of Buddhism as a living philosophy and with the special commitment to preserve and transmit important works from all the major Buddhist traditions.

If you would like more information or a copy of our mail-order catalog, please contact us at this address:

Wisdom Publications
199 Elm Street
Somerville, Massachusetts 02144 USA
Telephone: (617) 776-7416 • Fax: (617) 776-7841
Email: info@wisdompubs.org • www.wisdompubs.org

THE WISDOM TRUST

As a nonprofit publisher, Wisdom Publications is dedicated to the publication of fine Dharma books for the benefit of all sentient beings and dependent upon the kindness and generosity of sponsors in order to do so. If you would like to make a donation to Wisdom, please do so through our Somerville office. If you would like to sponsor the publication of a book, please write or e-mail us for more information.

Thank you.

Wisdom Publications is a non-profit, charitable 501(c)(3) organization and a part of the Foundation for the Preservation of the Mahayana Tradition (FPMT).